LEADERSHIP
FOR A
CHANGING
CHURCH

LEADERSHIP FOR A CHANGING CHURCH

Charting the Shape of the River

ROBERT D. DALE

Abingdon Press
Nashville

LEADERSHIP FOR A CHANGING CHURCH:
CHARTING THE SHAPE OF THE RIVER

Copyright © 1998 by Abingdon Press

This book is printed on recycled, acid-free, elemental-chlorine-free paper.

Library of Congress Cataloging-in-Publication Data

Dale, Robert D.
    Leadership for a changing church: charting the shape of the river
/Robert D. Dale.
        p.   cm.
    ISBN 0-687-01485-9 (pbk.: alk. paper)
    1. Christian leadership.   I. Title.
BV652.1.D334   1998   97-40921
262'.1—dc 21   CIP

Unless otherwise noted, Scripture quotations are taken from the *Holy Bible: New International Version.* Copyright © 1973, 1978, 1984 by the International Bible Society. Used by permission of Zondervan Bible Publishers.

98 99 00 01 02 03 04 05 06 07—10 9 8 7 6 5 4 3 2 1

MANUFACTURED IN THE UNITED STATES OF AMERICA

To my brother
Jim Dale (1944–1993),
who always seemed to know
the shape of the river,
the lay of the land,
and "the Code of the West"

CONTENTS

FOREWORD

A Parable of Hope for Frustrated Leaders **9**

PART ONE: Charting a Course for Third Millennium Leaders

1. Challenges of Leadership in a Postmodern
   World **13**
2. Religious Leaders for Tomorrow's Church **27**

PART TWO: Navigating the Theological Waters of Leadership

3. Values: Discovering Meaning Through
   Leadership Stance **47**
4. Versatility: Broadening Meaning Through
   Leader Styles **65**
5. Vision: Focusing Meaning Through
   Leader Strategies **81**

PART THREE: Setting Sail on the Leadership Voyage into the Future

6. Meaning-Making 101 **99**

AFTERWORD

A Parable of Hope for Future Leaders **119**

NOTES **121**

FOREWORD

A Parable of Hope for Frustrated Leaders: Learning the Shape of the River

In *Life on the Mississippi,* Mark Twain reports the navigational instructions he received from an experienced Mississippi riverboat captain. The captain explained that the look of the river changes constantly at night—depending on the moonlight. On clear nights, shadows hide snags and sandbars. When nights are inky and black, all shores blur into straight lines. But, on foggy and misty nights, the shores appear to have no shape at all. The possibilities seemed endless to Twain—so endless that he despaired of so many variations to master.

Twain complained bitterly about the complexity of the river's conditions: "Oh, don't say any more, please! Have I got to learn. . . five hundred thousand different ways? If I tried to carry all that cargo in my head it would make me stoop shouldered."

But the captain wisely quieted Twain's frustration: "You only learn the shape of the river, and you learn it with such absolute certainty that you can always steer by the shape that's in your head, and never mind the one that's before your eyes."[1]

Learn the shape of the river. Steer by the lasting shape that's in your head rather than the changing perspectives before your eyes. These are hopeful lessons for leaders.

PART ONE

CHARTING A COURSE FOR THIRD MILLENNIUM LEADERS

CHAPTER 1

Challenges of Leadership in a Postmodern World

Is it possible for leaders to lead today? Are there too many exceptions to the rules, five hundred thousand variations on the theme? The parable by Mark Twain in our foreword has a timely piece of advice for today's leaders. Learn the shape of the river! That's what effective leaders do—internalize the shape of the river. In other words, modern church leaders need navigational guidelines to help them scout out and chart the water levels and obstacles of the leadership river.

So what are contemporary leadership guides saying about the emerging shape of the river? Today's leadership river has at least three observable shapes: (1) a multilevel, "architectural" perspective on the basic shape of leadership, (2) a new definition or description that reframes leadership, and (3) a changing, shaping, postmodern context for leadership.[1] These three elements provide the contours for this chapter.

LEADER LITERACY

Leadership for a Changing Church: Charting the Shape of the River intends to expand leader literacy from a Christian perspective. So the early chapters are about what leadership is in today's world and in today's church. The middle chapters lay out the emerging shapes of contemporary religious leadership. And the final chapter describes how leaders will function in future congregations. The contours of contemporary leadership are explored throughout.

DIFFICULT CHALLENGES FOR LEADERS

Effective leaders understand our times. That's true, of course, in any age. In the Old Testament, when leadership of the kingdom of Israel was transferred from Saul's line to David's dynasty, warriors gathered at Hebron to fight in David's army. Among that host were 200 chiefs from the tribe of Issachar. Why did they join David? The historian notes that these men "understood the times" (1 Chronicles 12:32) and knew what Israel had to do. Leadership always has a where and when—a context. Without a clear understanding of leadership's times and contexts, leaders may mistakenly provide leadership for another place and time.

Like the earth's tectonic plates whose shifts cause earthquakes, new elements are challenging and radically reshaping the contemporary leadership equation. At least six large-scale trends at the end of the century continue to intensify and redefine the leadership arena as we approach the third millennium.[2]

1. The quantity of information and communication has mushroomed. Information can be instantaneously moved around the globe. Unfortunately, quantity of information and quality of communication aren't synonymous. Effective leaders, therefore, avoid simplistic communication as they flash information around the world.

2. Privacy is disappearing. Today's intimate, privileged information becomes tomorrow's headline. In this volatile context, the mystique of heroines and heroes disappears overnight. Still, leaders willingly risk media attack and public fickleness in order to serve.

3. Multinational organizations now transcend governmental boundaries. Leaders recognize and live comfortably amid the networked interconnectedness of today's world.

4. Ideologues abound in religious and political circles. Faith

14

communities are, consequently, becoming more and more brittle. But fair leaders state their beliefs without exploiting the biases and hatreds of others.

5. Expanding knowledge has made technical experts a dime a dozen. So leaders rely on good judgment as well as good information.

6. Leaders recognize that humankind has massive and sophisticated weaponry, threatening our world's future. Leaders call out the best in others and help people limit their destructive tendencies.

In summary, it is a new day. The demands of these trends, taken together, push the leadership envelope and require a new breed of leaders for this new day. The old approaches to leadership are becoming outmoded and increasingly ineffective. How can we understand our new opportunities to lead?

THE SHAPE OF LEADERSHIP

In our changing world, leadership is taking on a distinctive, multilayered shape. Many pastors have never taken formal classes in leadership and may have no explicit picture of leadership. To help us conceptualize and visualize the emerging issues in the field of religious leadership, let me introduce you to a new "architectural" model of leadership.

When leadership's architecture is sketched like a blueprint, it has at least three levels: stance, styles, and strategy. Each level is distinctive from but related to the other levels of leadership.

```
3. STRATEGY <———> ARTISTRY
        ^                ^
        ^                ^
    2. STYLES <———> ACTIONS
        ^                ^
        ^                ^
    1. STANCE <———> ATTITUDE
        ^                ^
        ^                ^
```

Stance provides the foundation for leadership's shape and structure. Stance, like a building's physical foundation, is hidden, below ground, and generally assumed to be solid. This mostly invisible, subterranean aspect of leadership is primarily shown by our attitudes and values. After all, how we treat others demonstrates the value we assign to them and reflects our attitudes directly. Stance raises why? and for whom? questions for leaders and spotlights servanthood,[3] integrity,[4] character,[5] spirituality,[6] and credibility.[7]

Historically, leader stance has at times become nearly as indistinct and difficult to define as Twain's dark river. Too often we have taken attitudes and values for granted and have neglected to inspect leadership's foundation—even in seminary or divinity school training. When clergy and other leaders fail, however, we see the fissures of flawed values and abusive attitudes. Fortunately, leader stance has become more of an overt issue recently.

Styles, the operational framework of leadership, is revealed by the observable pattern of actions or behaviors of leaders. Much like the shoals, snags, and sandbars of Twain's river during the light of day, leader styles are actually visible. Because of this tangibility, much of the training and theorizing about leadership zeroes in on leader styles. Style deals with what? and how? questions and concentrates on leadership practices,[8] the art of organizational orchestration,[9] making change from a values base,[10] and habits of effectiveness.[11] Leader style, always a topic of interest, has been the special focus of several recent treatments on historic leaders—Attila,[12] Jesus,[13] Sitting Bull,[14] and Lincoln.[15]

From a practical viewpoint, mission and morale form the two sides of the leadership coin.[16] Clarifying group mission and heightening group morale, two complementary leadership actions, are always needed in balance for groups to be well led and effective. Emphasizing mission and morale—in various ways, at various levels of intensity, and meeting various needs—creates an almost infinite range of leader styles. Versatility in blending mission and morale elements, then, is a necessary survival skill for today and tomorrow's effective leaders.

Strategy, the distinctive fit and finish of a structure, is the artistic element of leadership. When Ezra Pound described artists as the antennae of the race, he may also have been describing leaders-as-strategists. Strategists constantly narrow the focus of leadership to areas of personal and organizational strength and then work to accentuate those advantages. This most sophisticated and cerebral level of leadership's architecture centers in which? and when? questions and can be approached as a craft,[17] a hunter-gatherer lifestyle,[18] a skill to be taught and learned,[19] and a personal or congregational edge to be expanded.[20]

FROM MAKING THINGS TO MAKING SENSE

Leadership is currently being reshaped by a new, contemporary definition. For several centuries, descriptions of leadership have reflected industrial society's viewpoint. During the Industrial Age, leaders made things. Descriptions of leadership were mechanistic and drawn mostly from engineering and the physical sciences. We were producers—on assembly lines and factory floors as well as in offices and boardrooms. Operating in a fairly stable environment and making tangible things, leaders took actions and triggered reactions. We structured, commanded, and dominated, reflecting the influence-based definition of leadership from the Industrial Revolution. Frequently, leadership in the industrial society was a control-and-patrol process revolving around the "star of the show." We used the science of the day, mainly levers and hydraulics, to describe ourselves as leaders. We exerted pressure, and others reacted.

Now a new era and a fresh definition of leadership are emerging together. Machine language is being replaced by cyberimages; levers and hydraulics are giving way to computer networks; the physical sciences are stepping aside for the dynamism and liveliness of the biological sciences. Our information society calls for leaders who process data, recognize patterns, and interpret situations in fluid environments. Today's effective leaders must zoom nimbly down the information superhighway while dealing deftly with high-speed change. Leaders now function more as champions for the cause than as master managers of a hierarchy.

Consequently, an entirely different leadership paradigm is arising. Leaders now make sense rather than make things. More accurately, leaders make meaning.[21] Meaning sees the patterns, the ebbs and flows in a sea of information. Meaning puts a frame around the confusion of too much data and too many choices. In the Information Age, anyone who can make sense of our world for others becomes a de facto leader. This reminds us that leadership isn't limited to the head of the table or to titled persons who occupy corner offices. *Anyone* who makes sense is, for that moment in time at least, the group's leader.

What followers expect of leaders is shifting dramatically. In the agricultural era, we humans really were what we grew and ate, and during the industrially oriented age, we were what we produced and sold. But in an information-driven world, we are what we understand. This is especially good news for clergy. Clergy as leaders often felt slightly out of step with the Industrial Age's emphasis on making or producing tangible things. But leading by making sense of intangibles and tangibles is a function clergy understand. Meaning making is an arena Christian pastors and theologians have operated in from the beginning. We believe we have met and committed ourselves to the One who ultimately makes sense of our existence.

For practicing leaders, meaning is rooted in stance, demonstrated in style, and targeted by strategy. Contemporary leaders serve our followers in pathfinding roles—as data sorters, discerners, idea molders, symbol crafters, interpreters, translators, diagnosticians, storytellers, solution designers, stewards, ethicists, networkers, fellow pilgrims, and paradigm pioneers. These roles are no longer strictly managerial and centered on allocating what has been. The new leadership roles deal with meaning, mission, morale, and myth, and focus energy on "what is" and "what if."

WHEN THE RULES CHANGE

During roughly the last four hundred years, the science-based thinking style of the Industrial Age has dominated our culture. Especially in this century, leaders in the West have relied on logical, research-based, mostly left-brain thinking patterns. Too often this conventional approach was assumed to fit all of the estimated fifty thousand nonroutine decisions we make each day. A new connective [22] mind-set, prompted by the Information Age, is now emerging. A fresh approach, balancing the intuitive strengths of Greek and Hebrew thought forms as well as whole-brain solution finding skills, is beginning to assert itself.[23] Leaders realize that many things make sense that can't be explained with sequential, cause-effect reasoning. As a result, we're developing more symmetry and richness in our thinking patterns. After all, in the Information Age, leaders and followers are literally seeking a meeting of the minds.[24]

We live and lead between the times, between these two cognitive paradigms. The old industrial paradigm is waning, and a new information paradigm is emerging and overlapping with what has been. These interim conditions make our leadership challenge particularly difficult. Why? Because we manage amid the stability of enduring paradigms, but we must lead when we are between paradigms.[25]

LEADERSHIP IN A POSTMODERN WORLD

When our cultural pendulum swings from one paradigm to another, new and unfamiliar phenomena must be described. But that's not a simple challenge. How can we describe the shift from a modern outlook to a postmodern perspective? Defining a new paradigm typically begins with negatives. We know what some new thing isn't before we know what it is. We can usually draw stark contrasts earlier than we can make subtle comparisons. Consequently, only after new paradigms have established their identity can we fully describe them and deal with them comfortably and familiarly. Until then we fall back on negatives as we hammer out fuller and fairer definitions. Even comparing the terms *modern* and *postmodern* highlights our tendency to react and define against rather than for, when faced with new paradigms.

As modernity wanes and a postmodern paradigm emerges, leaders find ourselves in a frustrating paradigm overlap when out-of-the-box thinking is demanded. New definitions must be crafted for the postmodern leadership context. Given our between-the-times world, how can we describe the postmodern mind-set? Consider the three negatives below as a first step toward a more positive definition of leadership in this emerging era.

1. The postmodern world has *no rules.* By definition, new paradigms are always confusing and ill-defined. As yet there are no precise routines or customs for a postmodern world. Unfortunately, the broad descriptions we use for postmodernism don't create crisp definitions.

So, how can we lead in a ruleless epoch? Stephen Covey is correct in *Principle-Centered Leadership* when he argues that principles provide compasses for leaders.[26] To survive and thrive in a world without rules, leaders need principles based on character and integrity. Leaders who are self-defined help define their settings. For leaders, principles structure and inform a world without rules.

2. The postmodern world has *no speed limit.* Alvin and Heidi Toffler, in *Creating a New Civilization,* note that we live in the Third Wave of civilization. The First Wave, the Agricultural Age, endured seven or eight thousand years and has almost completely passed from the scene—except for a handful of primitive cultures. It was followed by the Second Wave, known as the Industrial Revolution. That industrial society, typified by a reliance on science, has endured for three or four hundred years but is currently ebbing away, especially in the

most highly industrialized nations. The Third Wave, known as the Information Age—which has been unfolding since the last quarter of the twentieth century and is driven by the electronic media—may run its course by 2020. The compression of change is obvious as each cultural wave shortens. The speed of change is so great that paradigms have shrunk from millennia to centuries to mere decades. We are hurtling helter-skelter toward the third millennium in a world without speed limits. The pace of change often leads to paradigm panic, triggering quick fixes to offset our fears and anxieties but rarely solving our problems.

A subtle shift in leadership development is already beginning to take this careening pace of change into account. In the early 1990s leadership literature began spotlighting vision less and values more. Values and character have a huge advantage for leaders in chaotic circumstances; they are portable and sustain us on the run. Values and character stabilize persons and organizations in high-speed environments.

3. The postmodern world has *no boundaries.* In the industrial society, information could be hoarded by leaders at the top of institutional hierarchies, in academia, or by resource-rich nations. But in an information society, information is available to all and becomes a leveling and leavening factor in the world. Information has now democratized power structures and superseded geographic barriers. National and institutional interests have been overridden by local and global concerns. Think globally, act locally is common advice for postmoderns.

In our boundary-transcending information society, leaders are persons who can sort through the glut of data and make some sense of our world. Creating contexts, linking ideas, and discovering patterns of meaning builds community—an arena of common sense. Community, especially local community, provides basic boundaries in our lives. And the community of others helps us live and lead in a boundaryless world.

Principles, values, community—these ingredients help define emerging paradigms. These foundational elements of the leadership equation enable us to act more positively in an increasingly negative culture.

NEW RULES AND NEW ROLES

New paradigms create new rules and new roles. The shift from an industrial society paradigm to an Information Age paradigm is making major changes in leadership's rule book. Fifteen significant changes within our world's new paradigm are suggested below:

From . . .	*To . . .*
Management	Leadership
Doing to	Discovering with
Factories	Homes
Standardizing	Customizing
Owners	Entrepreneurs
Skilled workers	Lifelong learners
Influence and levers	Meaning and symbolism
Assumes progress:	Assumes meaning:
If we build it,	If we understand it,
they will come . . .	they will know . . .
and buy it!	and value it!
Brawn	Brains
Position power	Personal power
National and institutional	Global and local
More gender-exclusive	More gender-inclusive
Metaphors from physics	Metaphors from biology
More scientifically/	More spritually/
technologically based,	artistically based,
rational	nonrational
Top-down decisions	Bottom-up decisions

In summary, these shifts in the cultural paradigm are showing up in three significant leadership trends. (1) Currently, there is more emphasis on values than vision in the emerging leadership literature. (2) Even though leadership has been and remains a pragmatic discipline, leader stance is currently being explored more actively than styles. (3) And the most fundamental change in leadership philosophy, overriding the other trends, is that making sense is now more central to defining leadership than simply making things.

WHETTING OUR APPETITE FOR MEANING

Making meaning is our contemporary leadership challenge, especially amid the current explosion of information. About one thousand books are published internationally each day. Nearly ninety-six hundred periodicals are issued in the United States alone each year. In terms of printed matter, knowledge doubles every eight years. In total, more information has been produced in the past thirty years than in the previous five thousand years. Our world is inundated with data; we're overloaded by information. No wonder some psychologists are talking about "information fatigue syndrome."

When a culture is drowning in information without contexts, leaders are required to guide us through the flooded rivers of words to the stable shores of personal and organizational meaning. Do you feel you can't keep up with your field? Have you ever nodded knowingly when a new book—one you've never heard of—is mentioned and you hoped against hope that no one would ask your opinion of the item? Did you try to explain something you thought you understood only to realize that you really didn't have a clue? Leaders help us move from facts to meaning, beyond knowing to understanding. More than simply knowing more, persons long to understand more. No wonder Gordon Allport describes humans' elemental thirst for understanding as "the appetite for meaning."[27] Another psychologist, Carl Jung, once described neurosis as a disease of souls who haven't found meaning.

PERSPECTIVES ON
POSTMODERN LEADERS

In our end-of-century, beginning-of-century world, leaders must practice their art with agility and craft. What are the shaping assumptions of the new leadership riverbed? What are the general outlooks required of contemporary leaders?[28] Here are a dozen actions effective leaders will take as we look toward the future.

1. Tomorrow's leaders will be quick-change artists. Future-oriented organizations are amoeba-like. They have a nucleus of core values and common mission, but their edges are constantly adapting, shifting, and changing. Speed, mobility, a project-orientation, and the ability to "turn on a dime" are now characteristics of effectiveness in the leadership arena.

2. Tomorrow's leaders will have our heart in our opportunities. Watching the clock and working toward Friday isn't the mode of leaders. Commitment is a key in any contemporary leader's success.

3. Tomorrow's leaders will use the accelerator relentlessly. Velocity is a survival skill in an impatient world. Traveling lighter and deciding quicker are absolute necessities. Conquering our fears is crucial for leaders. Our fears are the emotional darkroom where our negatives are developed. Effective leaders fail fast, master our fears, fix our errors on the spot, and move out again quickly.

4. Tomorrow's leaders will tolerate ambiguity as a fact of life. When asked how it feels to write a book, E. L. Doctorow replied: "It's like driving at night in a fog. You can only see as far as your headlights, but you can make the whole trip that way."[29] Contemporary organizations and leaders who can't deal with uncertainty are already dead in the water.

5. Tomorrow's leaders will be extremely entrepreneurial. Leaders act like owners—even when we are employees. We take our work personally. We discover what our audiences

need and consider it our sole responsibility to move our services closer to those key audiences and to do it now.

6. Tomorrow's leaders will learn forever. Current information and transferable skills keep leaders at the forefront of our organizations. We will increase our attractiveness and portability through lifelong learning. On the other hand, if we neglect to pull up our roots and repot ourselves periodically, we will have chosen to become and remain obsolete.

7. As tomorrow's leaders, we will hold ourselves accountable. As the boundaries within and between organizations become even more fluid, only those persons who forget about turf and concentrate on results will be able to do the right things at the right time for the right people.

8. Tomorrow's leaders will contribute. Recently, I saw an interesting church sign: "Jesus is returning soon. Look busy!" Apart from a variety of theological implications in that warning, leaders in the future will not be able to rely on busyness, tenure, or devotion. Only the value we add to our organizations each new day will count.

9. Tomorrow's leaders will envision ourselves as service centers. Leaders build direct, durable relationships with our primary audiences. We cultivate our contacts regularly. In short, effective leaders see ourselves as servants.

10. Tomorrow's leaders will take responsibility for our own morale. Where is it written that organizations must ensure the contentment of their employees? When we assume responsibility for our own outlook, we empower ourselves and increase our emotional resilience. Wounds, scars—even martyrdom— are part of life, but leaders don't wallow pessimistically in difficulties. Effective leaders refuse to ask others to give us self-sufficiency.

11. Tomorrow's leaders will grow constantly. Upgrading performance is demanded in a changing marketplace. Only those who stretch and transform our inner lives and outer skills will thrive. Making ourselves stronger for the future is the way to make a difference in the world of that future.

12. Tomorrow's leaders will solve problems. Change begets problems. The future will yield constant predicaments and challenges. Leaders are fixers rather than finger-pointers. Blame solves nothing—except to rob us of our power to face and deal with our problems. Organizations can't protect or rescue us, and leaders recognize that simple fact.

SHAPING THE LEADERSHIP RIVER

The world is changing dramatically. We have a fresh model for leaders. To make sense amid pervasive change, leaders use stance, styles, and strategy to form a functional architecture for their work of contemporary leadership. We have a new definition of leadership. In our Information Age, leaders are becoming meaning makers, linking the mundane to Mystery. The context for leadership is now informational, connective, and postmodern. The leadership river is rerouting itself and taking on novel shapes.

When Charles Dickens described his era as the best of times and the worst of times, he may have been predicting our time in the history of leadership. Our world needs leaders precisely because our world is changing so radically and so swiftly. Massive change makes our world the most challenging and threatening of times for leaders. This cultural earthquake also creates tremendous opportunities for leaders. We live in the worst time to be leaders, and we live in the best time to be leaders. Let's seize the day!

FROM THE SECULAR TO THE SACRED

Now, given these times and these shapes of the river in our broader culture, let us explore the religious dimensions of the new leadership arena. We've looked at the secular civilization; now let's consider congregational contexts for leadership.

CHAPTER 2

Religious Leaders for Tomorrow's Church

When my son was twenty-three, he gave some lectures on theology and art to a seminary class. His specific assignment was to describe the postmodern mind-set during a three-day teaching stint. At the end of his presentations, the professor—a seasoned and brilliant teacher—thanked him but lamented: "You've shown me that I'm preparing students for a world that no longer exists."

New paradigms always create translation challenges—especially for the church, a conserving institution by definition. The church has too rarely anticipated challenges and changes. We have been tempted to live in a world that no longer exists. Consequently, the future has too often surprised the church.

SO, WHAT'S NEXT?

What's coming next for the church, for your local church? Next is precisely the question. Only God knows, but there's no lack of guesses. These guesses generally follow the current trends in marketing. Years ago most local churches mirrored their community and ministered to a crossroads gathering point, a village, or a neighborhood. From a marketing perspective, these congregations functioned like family businesses in a mixed market. But times have changed.

While the mixed marketing approach still continues effectively in some settings, the trend in marketing is moving from mass marketing to niche marketing to particle marketing. Some, adopting the assumptions of mass marketing, foresee the next church as megachurch malls with everything members want for religion, recreation, and personal growth clustered under one roof.[1] Others speculate that future churches will adopt a small group, metachurch model akin to specialty shops that cater to narrow market niches. At the far extreme, some church members now demand particle marketing, an individualized approach to religion. This mail-order catalog approach strains attempts to build group fellowship and to program for broader constituencies.

Whatever the future holds for churches, we must prepare and plan for the next chapter in world history and church history now. Listen to Margaret Mead speak of the challenges of change: "Who will take trouble to warn of the doom to come unless some preferred future alternative is offered, either in steps that will avert that doom or in preparation for a next world. As doomsday is preached more vigorously, the more one is committed to a better world."[2] Next? Next! Whatever shape the next church takes, leaders must stretch their imaginations and anticipate as best they can what challenges loom on congregational horizons.

The next leadership questions for the church are fairly straightforward. How can guides of religious groups set the pace effectively in a postmodern world? What can religious leaders do to make meaning for a changing church in a changing world?

PACE AND PARADIGMS

The unprecedented and uncharted context of change is stirring today's church at several points. In the first chapter, I've already identified two distinctive dimensions of change in the postmodern world—the sheer pace of the changes that are careening past us plus the uncomfortable fact that we're caught between two paradigms of civilization. Together these changes imply a third—

and a largely unexplored—element of change in this between-the-times world.

YOUNG ENOUGH TO LEAD

Traditionally, we have counted on the past to interpret the future for us. After all, history told us how we got this way. We have relied on continuity within history to help us recognize and meet the demands of change. But does that cultural model serve our postmodern world? Does the past provide transitions into the future any longer?

The overwhelming pace of change has caused a unique situation. No longer does the past help us make sense of the present and future. Now, the future is more likely to introduce us to the past. In our world of fast-paced discontinuity, what is emerging helps us finally make sense of the world that is already passing from the scene.

Future-to-past retrospecting is a unique mode of meaning making. The New Testament, particularly Matthew's Gospel, hints at this different angle of historical interpretation. Although Matthew stresses even more strongly than the other Synoptic Gospel writers that Jesus fulfills the Old Testament messianic prophecies, he also strongly emphasizes the future as a filter for understanding the past. The overall apocalyptic theme of Matthew 24 as well as the specific parables of Matthew 25—the wise and foolish virgins (25:1-13), the talents (25:14-30), and the sheep and goat judgment (25:31-46)—demonstrate this future-based approach. Matthew reminds us that history is destination-drawn under the rule of God. It is important for meaning-making leaders to peer into the purposiveness of God's kingdom in order to escape the distracting chaos of the moment.

Anthropologist Margaret Mead saw this future-to-past phenomenon when she described three kinds of guidance for cultural change—postfigurative, cofigurative, and prefigurative.[3] Each culture has its own approach of adapting. In postfigurative settings the old guide the young. This was the customary pattern of traditionally paced cultures. Then, in more contemporary times, the pace of change escalated and enculturation became a team sport. In these cofigurative situations, the old and young guide each other. More recently, as a result of massive change, a new, prefigurative, interpretative paradigm has arisen out of necessity. In prefigurative cultures, the young guide the old. That, for good or ill, is increasingly our world.

Recently, I was consulting with an international ministry agency on leadership development needs. They were designing a new global initiative to train leaders. They asked me where they could find trainers and training materials for Information Age interpreters. I told them their challenge was to find people who were young enough to do the job. "Young enough?" they asked. At first they resisted this counterintuitive answer. After all, these were old hands at ministry, and they appreciated veterans who used seasoned approaches. But, to their credit, they quickly realized that a prime challenge of mastering new paradigms is unlearning the old ones—unless you are too young to have been marinated in the old paradigms in the first place.

Typical of the Information Age and reminiscent of the prophet Isaiah, little children—or, more likely, young adults—are sometimes now leading us (Isaiah 11:6). In the uncharted territories of paradigm shifts, even mostly postfigurative cultures are tending to become more prefigurative. Why? Because the young have less baggage from the old paradigm to carry with them.

A middle-aged friend of mine told me recently about his struggle to use the Internet. He had been frustrated by hardware, software, and his nagging discomfort with technology. With wry humor and a touch of shame he concluded his story by describing his four-year-old nephew who has his own Web page! So my midlife friend knew who his computer coach had to be. Major changes in cultural paradigms turn everything upside down and make leaders of otherwise unlikely persons who just happen to be plastic enough to understand a bit of what's happening around them. They can make sense. And that makes them leaders.

WHO ARE THE PLASTIC PARISHIONERS?

Plasticity, our flexibility in the face of change, is a key element in unlearning old models or in learning novel approaches. This plasticity may be less a challenge for younger persons since they have less to unlearn and a shorter distance to stretch into new paradigms. For example, older boosters have a greater stretch than younger busters.

Boosters —>   Learning the

Boomers ——>   New Paradigm of

Busters   ———>   the Information Age

The issue of paradigm plasticity has become even more of a concern for church leaders during the 1990s, since for the first time in the history of the planet, we have six generations alive simultaneously. If ways can't be found to bridge generational differences, generational conflict could well become a pivotal battleground for third millennium congregations as the young and old confront each other.

Are older leaders doomed to ineffectiveness or irrelevancy? Not if we are strong enough to bend flexibly and learn how to thrive in a postmodern world. Not if we can unlearn and learn afresh. But the re-education task will stretch old and young church leaders alike because none of us has ever before lived in this kind of world.

WHEN THE CHURCH'S CONTEXT CHANGES

Our new kind of world and our new kind of church call for new leadership approaches. At least three major changes are challenging the context of ministry and mission for today's church. We now lead (1) amid a new missionary environment, (2) with new definitions of success, and (3) in situations where former brothers and sisters in Christ see each other as opponents and demonize each other.[4]

First, the missionary context of the American church is a fairly new phenomenon. Formerly, church and ministers enjoyed a favored position and a positive image in society. Now, indifference toward the church is often the best we can hope for. In other circumstances, outright hostility has become the norm. In other words, Western society can no longer be automatically assumed to be friendly toward religion. That describes a new "post-something" mind-set for churches, variously called post-Christendom[5] or post-establishment.[6] This new era of the church requires a new approach to ministry, a missionary mind-set.

Recently, a Brazilian Baptist leader spoke to a gathering of American mission strategists. He thanked them for their efforts in establishing churches in his country a century ago. Then, with tears in his eyes, he pled: "Don't forget the United States!" Some of these missiologists were momentarily stunned, but they quickly saw the new reality of their ministry arena. No longer can Christian churches in the West assume a dominant position in their communities. We now live and lead in a missionary culture here in the United States too.[7] The pluralism of our world and the shifting cultural paradigms have expanded our ministry challenge and forced us to acknowledge that we are now missionaries in our own communities.

Second, success is now defined differently too. In the Industrial Age success was often a matter of counting. How many? How much? In the modern church, the most tangible items were nickels and noses—so we calculated both and judged our success by the totals. After all, numbers were easy measures of success and progress, and science provided objective methods to evaluate success. Then the paradigm shifted, and success became more slippery. Millions can be weighed and measured, but Mystery can't. The Information Age has pushed us to look for different ways to identify intangibles and to judge their meaningfulness.

Third, the traditional church found its demons in the world. In the Information Age, the threat of change in the church has brought the foes closer to home. Change, often viewed as a threat to traditional forms of faith, causes some churches to sprint frantically back into the past in search of security. In denominational family after denominational family, the opponents have become former brothers and sisters in Christ. Sadly, we are seeing the demonization of the church. Currently, conflict—the dark underbelly of change—has labeled and accused persons in our own faith family as nonbelievers. When new paradigms arise, we may see those who operate in a different paradigm as outsiders and zealously defend ourselves against them.

WAVES AND TRIBES
OF JUDEO-CHRISTIANITY

Another way to examine the change that confronts the church is to explore how cultural paradigm shifts have paralleled the history of religion. The Tofflers have identified three waves of civilization in agricultural, industrial, and informational eras.[8] Bailey has observed how science has paralleled the various cultural eras. When the nomads adopted an agricultural lifestyle, place became paramount. During the Industrial Age, pace—the cadence of clocks and calendars—dominated that mind-set. Now, the information world emphasizes pattern, the bigger pictures in the culture.[9] Has Judeo-Christian religion in some way paralleled these epochs of cultural history too? Has each wave of civilization been met by a matching change in the forms of religion?

Judaism was *a tribal religion* in its beginnings during the Agricultural Age. God established a covenant with the Hebrew tribes and called on them to become a redemptive minority to the majority of the world. When Christianity emerged out of the Hebrew foundations, it carried on that redemptive calling with essentially a tribal mind-set. Then, with the Renaissance and Reformation, the Judeo-Christian tradition broadened into *a religion of tribes* with splintering in both the Roman and Protestant branches of the family tree throughout the Industrial Revolution. Currently, the arrival of the information society has seen further splintering within religious families toward their extreme expressions and has helped create an even greater awareness of world religions, cults, and sects. Because of these splinterings, we are now seeing *tribes of religions* defining themselves in our pluralistic ministry arenas. From tribal religion to a religion of tribes to tribes of religions, the waves of civilization wash over faith families too. Effective leaders need unusual depth and breadth in order to make sense of and to excel in this new ministry environment.

TRENDS OF THE TIMES

Amid this "tribes of religions" era, Jeff Woods has described seven congregational megatrends affecting the contemporary church. Each of these trends reframes challenges for the leaders of today's churches. Let me simply list the trends and then comment on the leadership trend only:

Evangelism—from mass to relational
Education—from tribal to immigrant
Missions—from surrogate to hands-on
Spirituality—from reasonable to mysterious
Leadership—from official to gifted
Programming—from segmented to holographic
Planning—from secondary to primary

Woods's fifth congregational megatrend reminds us that leadership in an Information Age isn't a matter of status, prominence, position, or authority. The official marks of the old leader paradigm count for less and less these days. What matters is who can make sense out of our changing church. People who are meaning-making leaders have a gift to give the church—even if they have never been ordained, given a title, or assigned a corner office. By making common sense, gifted believers will lead the next church from pews and/or pulpits, from the streets and/or the sanctuaries.

LEADERSHIP AS A PERFORMING ART

Making meaning is the central task in a connective church that is increasingly systemic, intercultural, multilingual, and cross-generational. What can Information Age church leaders do to lead as we navigate the transition from making things to making meaning? When the leadership metaphors are switching from mechanical to mystical, how do we behave? As the pace and scope of change adjusts from incremental to transformational, how do meaning makers function as leaders in congregational contexts?

Basically, directors for the emerging church fill three constructive roles and make leadership into a performing art. We serve our constituencies as (1) community builders, (2) team orienteers, and (3) group anchors. Each of these roles stages sequential acts in the leadership play and, taken together, make up the larger script for the "story" leaders to tell.

NEW LEADER ROLES

Community Builders
Team Orienteers
Group Anchors

To implement these nontraditional leadership roles, leaders use a tried-and-true leadership methodology in a fresh way. To develop, anchor, and orient congregational life, contemporary leaders use stories as their mechanism for meaning making. Building on the central message from their parables of possibility, they create the connection between communication and community. Let me briefly describe each of these roles and then point you to the final chapter, Meaning-Making 101, for a more detailed discussion of these distinctive roles of Information Age meaning makers.

BUILDING FAITH COMMUNITIES

As community builders, leaders help link persons and ideas into meaningful, connective patterns.[10] In a mobile world and a changing church, community is tough to find. Leaders realize how important community is. We help people who don't know each other become acquainted. Connecting to a community is often the initial challenge for a new leader. Without a community, a leader is merely a talking head.

Additionally, we are community-building, pattern finders in the world of ideas. Leaders link the old and the new in order to lend continuity and to make sense of our worlds. We weave varied, almost random pieces of information into larger frameworks that mean something. Leaders provide the spiritual and emotional software programs for our church.

Such guides know that leadership always has a where, a community context. Uniquely, each community context or culture has its own "mother tongue," its distinctive, "nuanced language" for expressing its stories of meaning.[11] A regional context, for instance, can be heard in its own accents, smelled in restaurants, and observed in faith styles too.

Take only one geographic area of the United States as an example—the South. John Shelton Reed, Director of the Center for the Study of the American South in Chapel Hill, North Carolina, describes three Souths—Dixie, the Southeast, and Down Home.[12] Dixie contains the remnants of the Old Confederacy and lives on mainly as an artifact of history. But the echoes of Dixie's social and racial attitudes can be heard and seen faintly on Sundays at 11:00 A.M. The Southeast refers to the commercial centers of the new South, symbolized by "Hotlanta" and the Sun Belt. Office and industrial parks, shopping centers, and national retail stores along the region's interstate highways are visible signs of globalism. Megachurches using television and easy interstate access put religious faces on the entrepreneurial bent of the Southeast. "Down Home" is characterized by common folkways, memories, and values. "Blue-line" highways, small-scale cottage industries, and mom and pop businesses mark Down Home. The heterogeneous "family chapels" common to rural areas, villages, and neighborhood churches often reflect "Down Home-ness."

Leaders in distinctive, regionalized community contexts must speak the mother tongue of that context in order to tell the gospel story and to build community effectively. Additionally, we are often challenged also to speak in a minor key in order to bridge the subsystems of the larger community context. When massive cultural change occurs, leaders are stretched to the limit as translators of and communicators within communities.

ORIENTING FAITH TEAMS

Do you know what a reader of a flat map looks for first? He or she looks for the north arrow. To make sense of a map, an orientation point is fundamental. Only then do such additional features as scale, grids, symbols, and colors become most relevant. Without north, maps make no sense.

Leaders connect with our constituents and then help point the way. Showing the way is the second basic role of leaders. As team orienteers, leaders point to true north. Like navigators, we orient our team for the journey. Good leaders don't suffer from intention deficit disorder. We recognize reality and remain focused on it.

Recently, I asked a young rock climber how he oriented himself to and prepared to scale a rock face he had never seen before. The process he described fascinated me. First, he studied the face of the rock, visualizing his route to the top. He looked for features of the face where wedges could be placed for stability and for leverage. Then he pictured himself scaling the rock. He even plotted a timetable. For three days prior to the climb, he thought about the challenges of the climb, psyched himself up, and trained mentally and physically for the actual ascent. The day before the climb, he rested and memorized where gear could be stored for camps and for the descent. Then on the day of the ascent, he attacked the rock and climbed. Difficult or dangerous tasks require the most orientation and the best planning.

By the way, this young climber mentioned an element of climbing I hadn't really considered. How is climbing with a partner or a party unique? Teamwork. You develop a bond as well as a rhythm of climbing with a partner. Assuring partners of safety removes fear from the minds of climbers. Teamship becomes even more crucial when safety or even life itself is on the line.

When the directions of the compass can be sorted out, the details of maps begin to fall into place. Consequently, Max DePree claims that a leader's first responsibility is to define reality.[13] Remember those "You are here" notes on directories of public buildings? They define our location, our spatial and spiritual reality. When you know precisely where you are and can thereby orient yourself accurately, then you can determine what makes sense for you and your team. In this way leaders point to ultimate reality and give hope. Leaders provide spiritual and moral compasses in times of high-speed change.

ANCHORING FAITH GROUPS

As the group anchors, leaders deal calmly with the anxiety and panic that change inevitably brings to congregations. In spooked groups especially, leaders function nonanxiously as circuit breakers[14] who stand fast, and, by staying steady, help the group regain its equilibrium. Leaders try to keep their heads when others are losing theirs amid turbulence. Rather than overreacting, they slow the rush, clear the muddle, calm uncertainty, and mediate tension. Most important, leaders don't become carriers who infect the rest of the body with the short circuits of panic and anxiety. They resist paradigm panic, the temptation to fix things before they understand whether or not they're broken.

Meaning isn't made in a vacuum. By word and deed, leaders help our groups find a toehold in reality in order to move ahead. Building a community is the first role of an interpreter. Orienting the team is the leader's second role. Defining our own values and vision within—and even apart from—that community is our third role. The first role is communal and external; the second role is subgroup and directional; and the third role is personal and internal.

STORIES TOLD, STORIES LIVED

In an Information Age and for the "next church," leaders embody our central message. Leaders choose a core story and then model its message, becoming guides in both word and work. These stories focus on personal identity within broader community. Consequently, leader stories link inclusive we-and-they messages. Beginning with a common feature of what is known to the communicator and the community, the story unfolds and expands as the guide-follower relationship deepens. Leaders move followers from the familiar to the future by making sense of our past, present, and future.

Effective interpreters paint pictures for our followers and then practice what we preach. Jesus told stories and lived them out. Jesus told thirty to forty parables of the kingdom of God, comprising one-third of all his recorded teachings. Additionally, he embodied elements of the kingdom in enacted parables like the Last Supper and the Triumphal Entry. Jesus painted meaning-full pictures with words.

Other historical leaders have used the same mechanism of message and modeling. Patrick Henry energized his fellow patriots in 1775 before the American Revolution with his fiery "Give me liberty, or give me death" challenge at St. John's Church in Richmond. Lincoln's image-rich Gettysburg Address launched a national healing process after the Civil War. Franklin Roosevelt assured a shaken nation that we had "nothing to fear but fear itself." Martin Luther King, Jr. painted powerful word pictures about the outcomes of the civil rights movement in his "I Have a Dream" speech.

In the third millennium, leaders serve as storytellers for our groups. The stories we tell signal what makes sense to us, and what we have found meaningful for us. What we carry with us is a token of what we've found meaning-full.

Here's a clue to what you find meaningful. What would you carry with you if you had to travel light? Who travels lighter, for instance, than soldiers who are going into battle? In that circumstance, only essentials are taken along. Tim O'Brien, award winning fiction author for his stories on Vietnam, recalls what members of his platoon carried with them: photos, Bibles, even drugs. But, mostly they carried their stories—stories of connections, communities, and meaning. "Stories are for joining the past to the future. Stories are for those late hours in the night when you can't remember how you got from where you were to where you are. Stories are for eternity, when memory is erased, when there is nothing to remember except the story."[15] Our stories graphically convey our personal and communal meanings.

LEADERS AS DREAM WEAVERS

As community builders, team orienteers, and group anchors, Information Age leaders use stories to explain life and to weave the dreams of our networks. As interpreters we energize others by putting the heart hungers of our constituents into narrative form. In short, we find language for the longings our followers are feeling but can't fully articulate. When we state the search of our collective spirits succinctly, we become dream weavers. In like fashion, Jesus used stories as looms for meaning and action. When he created an interactive community of disciples, he did not say anything to them without using a parable (Mark 4:39). Jesus told stories of meaning for his day.

OUR SEARCH FOR MEANING

Meaninglessness is the central dilemma for humans in our contemporary world, according to Viktor Frankl. Echoing

Nietzsche, Frankl claims, however, that persons with a "why" to live can cope with almost any "what" in life.[16] Causes outweigh circumstances.

The Bible consistently points questioners and seekers toward the "why" of life. How can the powerless find hope? The book of Esther reminds us that ultimately God controls history. Why do bad things happen to good people? Job probes ways to deal with undeserved suffering and assures us of the presence of God. Is life worth living? Ecclesiastes counsels a hopeful reverence for God and an appreciation of prudent lifestyles amid the uncertainties of life. Where can we find God? John's Gospel shows us that Jesus revealed God to all who would believe in him. Throughout, the Bible points us to God who makes sense for us.

WHEN MEANING TOOK ON FLESH

Christian theology interprets meaning in life based squarely on the person and work of Jesus Christ. When the Word—our ultimate meaning in life—took on flesh (John 1:14), meaning making became the basic ministry of all believers. This ministry is modeled in the works-to-words rhythm of John's Gospel, the editorial page on Jesus' life. That movement or rhythm is demonstrated graphically in the seven signs or miracles of John with each miracle followed by an exposition of meaning. To illustrate, in John 6 Jesus fed five thousand when he multiplied a little boy's lunch (John 6:1-15) and then described himself as the bread of life (John 6:35). The miraculous work or sign provides the occasion for Jesus to become a meaning-making leader.

Postmodern interpreters in congregations have opportunities for meaning making too—but not without challenges. It's almost as if a few centuries ago science cut a deal with faith. According to the agreement, science would deal with the real world, and the church would deal with matters of the spirit. Unfortunately, the church lost the culture to science. "If you can't see it, it isn't real" and "What can't be measured, doesn't exist" became the way we dealt with modern reality in the West until recently. The postmodern mind-set and the new science have opened fresh possibilities. Meaning-hungry issues announce themselves everywhere in today's world. Visit your local bookstore. Angels, near-death experiences, and broadly defined spirituality are featured as "hot topics" with shelves of new titles. Meaning is a universal human search. Interestingly, our postmodern world is asking questions for which the church has answers. Our time for exciting leadership and meaning making has come.

DO-IT-YOURSELF MEANING MAKING

Ultimately, meaning making is a do-it-yourself process. Meaning is always personalized, contextualized, and customized. Meaning is personalized because what makes sense to me may not make sense to you. It is contextualized because settings, systems, and situations provide frameworks for connecting meaning across persons and groups. Meaning is customized because you and I tailor and time the applications of the sense we make of life to our special needs, opportunities, and circumstances. Leaders as meaning makers are "do-it-yourselfers" who create a connective process of the guide's story, the follower's needs, and the leader and follower's community.

What makes sense to people is sometimes individual, sometimes a group experience. In his classic novella *A River Runs Through It*, Norman Maclean weaves his family's saga around the metaphor of fishing, launching the book with the statement that "in our family, there was no clear line between religion and fly fishing."[17] As the story concludes, the father, an aging Presbyterian pastor, and his two sons go fishing together again—for what turns out to be the final time. The sons fish the trout stream aggressively, but their father, unable to wade the river anymore, stakes out a spot on the bank and fishes from there. When the older son returns to his father's fishing place, he finds his father completely at peace, reading the prologue to John's Gospel in his Greek New Testament. The old pastor muses, "In the part I was reading it says the Word was in the beginning, and that's right. I used to think water was first, but if you listen carefully you will hear that the words are underneath the water . . . the water runs over the words. . . . Eventually, all things merge into one, and a river runs through it."[18] The sequence is important, isn't it? Meaning emerges first, and then the waters of leadership carry the meaning along, no matter whether the context is individual or corporate.

TO THE KINGDOM FOR THIS TIME

In an Information Age, religious leaders and ministry groups have an open door for meaning making. Our theology speaks to our need for meaning; our theology speaks from our discovery of meaning. Belief leads to behavior. Our ministry actions show what we consider to be meaningful. In fact, how we leaders behave may be the best clue to our operational theology.

Effective church interpreters are forced in advance to clarify their theology and to make their stance, styles, and strategy second nature. Why? Because the church and the world are moving so fast that we must do ministry on the run. Frequently, faith's attempts to find meaning are as much implicit as explicit, as intuitive as rational, and as often discovered in action as through reflection. Donald E. Nanstad, pastor of Our Savior Lutheran Church in East Boston, makes this point graphically: "You don't always have time to think through the situation and carefully define your theological reasons for taking action. But if the ball is thrown at you, you do everything you can to catch it."[19] Well, history has thrown the leadership ball into our court. Let's not fumble the ball! Let's make meaning and lead!

PART TWO

NAVIGATING THE THEOLOGICAL WATERS OF LEADERSHIP

CHAPTER 3

Values: Discovering Meaning Through Leadership Stance

A leader's stance provides a foundation for leadership. Growing out of our attitudes, values, spirituality, and character, stance undergirds our efforts to set the pace in groups and to interpret situations. Jesus described leaders' fundamental attitude in the most comprehensive statement he made about leadership (Mark 10:35-45). In this important passage, Jesus made servanthood the basis for leadership stance.

Stance is the below-ground element of leadership. It's usually unseen, unexamined, and taken for granted. Think of how you approach a house or public structure. Do you evaluate the foundation and footings? If you're like most of us, you assume the structure is architecturally solid and never give a thought to the foundation. Ordinarily, our attention is aimed at the above-ground aspects of structures. Until—until structural flaws are revealed by cracked walls and sagging floors. Then we take the soundness of the foundation seriously. It can be tragic when leaders take both their stance toward leadership and their attitude toward the led for granted. Attitudes, character, values, credibility, and spirituality are the raw materials of stance and are crucial for leaders who intend to last in a connective world.

A WORD FROM OUR SPONSOR

Where leadership stance is concerned, the Mark 10 passage is *the* word from our Sponsor. Unfortunately, this passage is often misapplied. With servant leadership gaining more current attention in literature and practice, it is interesting to hear serious leaders confess their difficulty in applying a servant *style* of leadership. Mark 10 clarifies this point for us. What Jesus describes in this passage is stance rather than style, basic attitudes rather than behavior patterns. Stance precedes style. Stance undergirds a literal smorgasbord of styles. Mark 10 deals with a basic perspective and with the underlying attitudes we bring to leadership opportunities more than any specific style of leadership.

WHO'S THE BOSS?

A prevalent attitude in our culture reveals a misplaced value about leadership attitudes. Few persons in this postmodern world want to be servants. Rather, we prefer to be bosses.

"Who's the boss?" is more than reruns of an old TV series. It's a fundamental theological question for modern church leaders. Apparently, it's a question we should be asking, especially with the recent debate in some circles about the authority of the pastor. In that debate, when the "who's the boss" question is asked, too often pastors reply, "I am. I'm the boss, the overlord. I call the shots in this church."

But, as is often the case, culture and Scripture are at odds. The New Testament gives a strikingly different and terribly old-fashioned answer to the "who's the boss" inquiry. The New Testament states plainly: "Jesus Christ is Lord" (Philippians 2:11). It's not necessarily the emphasis today's church leaders want to hear. We want the authority; we like to be overlords. But the theological principle is clear: Lordship always precedes overlordship. Christian leaders operate from a basic truth: We lead for the Lord's sake and in order to introduce God's kingdom in the church and to the world.

As church leaders, we are servants of Christ in attitude and action. Jesus Christ is boss, an affirmation and stance that provides a foundation for developing leadership styles and strategies. It is an indictment of our time, our culture, and particularly our vocation that when we encounter a servant we are surprised and chastened.

SURPRISED BY SERVICE

One warm evening in May of 1991, Jeff Wisdom and I settled into a booth in a restaurant in Norfolk, Virginia and ordered supper. I don't remember what we ate. In a way, the meal itself was almost beside the point. We were there to talk, and talk we did—before our food arrived and until it was all gone. Jeff and I have a good time when we talk—good and honest and interesting talk. Other than the enjoyment of our conversation, not much else was noteworthy about our hour or two together—except for the service. Our waitress was especially thoughtful and attentive. Nothing we requested seemed to be any trouble at all, and most of the time she anticipated our wishes even before we asked. As we prepared to leave, we left a generous tip. But suddenly money didn't seem quite adequate to say thanks to this unusually helpful waitress. On an impulse, I reached into my shirt pocket, took out a business card, and wrote on the back, "Thank you for being so nice to us." I left the card with the tip and forgot the incident—for more than two full years.

My secretary gave me one of those little pink telephone slips with a call to be returned. The note was marked simply "Lee Jacobson, Norfolk." I assumed I was calling back one of our Virginia pastors, although I couldn't place the name. A female voice answered the phone, and, after a moment of confusion, I suddenly realized Lee Jacobson was a woman. She told me that I wouldn't remember her and that she didn't really know me either—except for a business card with a thank-you message written on the back and left on a restaurant table in Norfolk. Then I remembered supper with Jeff. I told her that I didn't usually leave my card, but that Jeff and I were especially grateful for the way she served our table. She replied that she ordinarily didn't receive or keep thank-you notes—but apparently needed a kind word the day Jeff and I ate at the restaurant where she worked.

Then she told me her story. Lee is a Christian, active in the choir and Bible study program of her Catholic church. She had taken a job as a waitress while she wrote a book on the sexual abuse of children. Her book *Pitterpat*[1] has been published now, and is receiving good reviews. While moving to another apartment a few days before, she had found my card. Lee called to offer a review copy of her book and to ask if Virginia Baptists had any ministry efforts to deal with the tragic issue of child sexual abuse. We had a spirited conversation about helping children.

Does it strike you as strange that we Christians are surprised by service—in restaurants or in churches? Maybe the Lee Jacobsons are reminders of a lost ministry theme. Perhaps these rare servants are a goad for consciences grown insensitive to a basic teaching of Jesus. Servanthood describes the foundational spirit of Christian leadership.

HE CAME TO SERVE

We aren't fans of personal slavery in twenty-first-century America, are we? Our world favors freedom, independence, being our own bosses. So when our modern ears hear that strange word from our Sponsor in Mark 10, we can usually find a way to turn a deaf ear toward the alien message—and even the Messenger.

The words about servanthood are fairly familiar. We have heard them before. But have we really heard them—heard them with enough clarity and conviction to act on them? What about you? Are you tempted to look for ways to ignore Jesus' plain description and its demands on your stance as a leader? Are you ready to explore the implications of the attitude you have about the people you lead?

"You know that those who are regarded as rulers of the Gentiles lord it over them, and their high officials exercise authority over them. Not so with you. Instead, whoever wants to become great among you must be your servant, and whoever wants to be first must be slave of all. For even the Son of Man did not come to be served, but to serve, and to give his life as a ransom for many." (Mark 10:42-45)

Will you go on a journey with me? Let's walk back through the Bible's record of servanthood. What exactly do the Old and New Testaments tell us about who's the boss? There's nothing casual about the lordship issue. The question in the Scriptures is never whether we will worship and serve something or someone. Augustine had it right. We are restless souls until we rest in God. Who's the boss? We are always committing to something or to someone. Is our boss Jesus Christ the Lord? We must settle the lordship question before we can face the challenges of overlordship fortified with power.

THE HEBREWS' VIEW OF SERVANTHOOD

God's people in the Old Testament remembered serving others—and they didn't like it. The title of Clyde Edgerton's novel aside, the Hebrews never wanted to go "walking across Egypt" again. One experience of slavery was quite enough, thank you. The Exodus experience left a permanent scar on the Hebrews' psyche. As far as the Hebrews were concerned, Egypt was the low point of Old Testament history. A little bit of making bricks without straw had gone a long way and was impossible to erase from memory. The Israelites never forgot how demeaned they felt as slaves in Egypt, and they had no yen to become anyone's servants again.

But God refused to stop reminding his people that they were called to be a servant nation, a redemptive minority amid the nations. And the Hebrews knew well their own customs. They saw that the treaties of the ancient Near East called for two parties—one in the role of exclusive sovereign or master and the other in the role of vassal or servant.

One exclusive master and some committed servants quickly

became the measure of the Jehovah and Israel relationship in the Promised Land, a region overflowing with gods—all of whom wanted to claim the hearts of the newcomers lately arrived from Egypt and wandering beyond the Jordan River. While the Israelites were tempted to follow many gods, they were told repeatedly that the God who had saved them from Pharaoh was a jealous God who accepted no rivals. When the exclusive God gave the commandments, he answered that pesky "who's the boss" question again:

> "I am the LORD your God, who brought you out of Egypt, out of the land of slavery. You shall have no other gods before me. You shall not make for yourself an idol. . . . You shall not bow down to them or worship them; for I, the LORD your God, am a jealous God. . . . You shall not misuse the name of the LORD your God. . . . Remember the Sabbath day by keeping it holy." (Exodus 20:1-8)

Who's the boss? The One who loved us enough to rescue us. The One who has shown he deserves our unrivaled devotion. The One whose name stands above all other claims. The One who created us in the first place.

If God is our boss, then what's left? Service. We are called to serve him alone. However, in the Promised Land the Hebrews didn't serve their jealous God, and chaos erupted. The judges turned Israel back to the One God time after time. And, time after time, the Hebrews fell in love with rival suitors. Notice how the Promised Land brimmed with gods.

> Again the Israelites did evil in the eyes of the LORD. They served the Baals and the Ashtoreths, and the gods of Aram, the gods of Sidon, the gods of Moab, the gods of the Ammonites, and the gods of the Philistines. . . . The Israelites forsook the LORD and no longer served him. (Judges 10:6)

So God refused to save them any longer. He allowed Israel to be conquered and oppressed. Service is always a decision, isn't it? They had chosen their fate. In the Old Testament world, you could be a slave either by circumstance or by choice. The Jew knew full well how circumstances made people into slaves: lose a war and become a slave, fail to pay debts and become a slave, be born into a subjugated family or nation and become a slave.

But they also knew that service could be a choice. The option of ministering to the world as a Servant Nation is offered again in Isaiah (Isaiah 42:1-4; 49:1-6; 50:4-9; 52:13–53:12). So the Hebrews could voluntarily give themselves to slavery. Over time, some were forced into slavery by circumstance, but only a few chose to enter servanthood freely. The Hebrews stiffened their necks and said, "Don't expect me to go back to Egypt again."

GREEK PERSPECTIVE ON SERVANTHOOD

The Greeks, whose ideas provided some of the backdrop for the Christian drama, hated servanthood for themselves too. They saw slavery as part of the natural fabric of life—and hoped it wouldn't get woven into their personal lives. According to the Greeks, some were born to nobility and others to subjugation. Slavery was for others—the vanquished, the weak, the prisoner. Remember when the New Testament begins, the Israelites are again dealing with defeat and trying to escape inferior status.

SERVANTHOOD IN THE NEW TESTAMENT

Judeo-Christian backgrounds don't exactly model servanthood, do they? But, if contemporary Christian leaders want to be like Christ, we must take servanthood seriously. The loftiest description of Christ in the New Testament is the hymn fragment from Philippians with its stark declaration of the slavery of Jesus:

Your attitude should be the same as that of Christ Jesus:
Who, being in very nature God,
    did not consider equality with God something to be grasped,
but made himself nothing,
    taking the very nature of a servant,

being made in human likeness.
And being found in appearance as a man,
   he humbled himself
   and became obedient to death—
      even death on a cross!
Therefore God exalted him to the highest place
   and gave him the name that is above every name,
that at the name of Jesus every knee should bow, .
   in heaven and on earth, and under the earth,
   and every tongue confess that Jesus Christ is Lord,
   to the glory of God the Father.
                          (Philippians 2:5-11)

ATTITUDE PRECEDES ACTION

Attitudes set the stage for action. In fact, the values of leaders are revealed in our actions. Church leaders' values are demonstrated particularly (1) in the identity of their Master and (2) by their treatment of their members. What we do as leaders grows out of who—and Whose—we are. Three attitudes are typical of Christian servants, according to Mark 10. Let's examine each of these three servant attitudes.

A LORDSHIP ATTITUDE

In Mark 10, Jesus contrasted the Gentile pattern of leaders lording it over their followers with the Christian approach of service. " Not so with you" (v. 43) signaled clearly that being the boss was not the supreme goal of Christ's disciples. First lordship, then overlordship is the foundation Jesus laid down for Christian leaders.

Leaders need a lordship audit. There's nothing theoretical in asking, "Who's the boss?" Those of us who are entrusted with setting the pace with others must be clear about where our allegiances are placed. We are called to show publicly to Whom we have pledged our allegiance. We voluntarily give our lives to Christ, and let him shape our attitudes.

Symbols are important clues to attitudes in leadership. Exodus 21:5-6 depicts the public ceremony commemorating voluntary servitude. Note the symbol of the pierced ear.

"If the servant declares, 'I love my master and my wife and children and do not want to go free,' then his master must take him before the judges. He shall take him to the door or the doorpost and pierce his ear with an awl. Then he will be his servant for life." (Exodus 21:5-6)

Doors and ears are interesting images in the Bible. The threshold of a Hebrew home was a sacred place; the ear was the physical entry point for commands. The volunteer slave stood on the threshold, and an awl was thrust through his ear into the door. The symbolism of the ceremony was two-fold. Not only was the pierced ear a mark of slavery in the ancient world, but the servant was also literally attached to his master's household—or at least to its doorpost.

Wade Paris recalls a vivid story of servanthood from his childhood in McNairy County, Tennessee. Wade knew old Doc Sanders, a country doctor who was identified by his simple lifestyle, shabby clothes, and long prayers in church. One day Wade made an unkind remark about Doc Sanders in his father's hearing. Wade's father corrected him quickly. "Son, you don't understand Doc and how wealthy he is. When Doc was younger, he literally broke his own health by taking care of his patients. He always lived frugally. But he gave generously to others and to his church. He paid for much of his church's building, although few people knew it. And Doc has paid college tuition for many young people who otherwise couldn't go."

I admire Wade's father's explanation. "I was ashamed. Doc was living like Jesus, and I was making fun of him." It sounds like old Doc Sanders knew who his Boss was and had adopted an attitude of lordship, doesn't it?

A PARTNERSHIP ATTITUDE

Leaders also need a partnership attitude. Review Mark 10:41-45 again. Jesus heard a special request from two of his disciples. The sheer nerve of that request made the other disciples angry and divided the Twelve. With the breach evident, Jesus called the group together and literally put his team back together. He knew two would not likely do the work of twelve. Even ten of twelve wouldn't do. Service and leadership require full partnership.

We serve among many other servants. Jesus demonstrated servanthood toward his partners in ministry on another occasion when he washed their feet, an act of Oriental courtesy. Servanthood is symbolized by towels and basins, according to John's Gospel:

> Having loved his own who were in the world, he now showed them the full extent of his love. The evening meal was being served, and the devil had already prompted Judas Iscariot, son of Simon, to betray Jesus. Jesus knew that the Father had put all things under his power, and that he had come from God and was returning to God; so he got up from the meal, took off his outer clothing, and wrapped a towel around his waist. After that, he poured water into a basin and began to wash his disciples' feet, drying them with the towel that was wrapped around him. (John 13:1b-5)

By definition, partners serve each other. I saw a dramatic example of a service partnership in mid-1992. Our family friend was seriously ill with multiple malignancies. During the summer I visited with her in Wake Forest, North Carolina, for what I feared would be our final time together. We talked about University of North Carolina basketball, one of Ruth's favorite conversation topics. Ruth's regard for Dean Smith, the head basketball coach at Carolina, was without limit. She had followed his successful coaching career and had met him at church several times on visits to see her daughter in Chapel Hill.

As I drove back home to Richmond after our conversation, I

realized what would lift Ruth's spirits—a contact from Dean Smith! The question was how to enlist Coach Smith's help. So, I wrote him. I told him a member of the Carolina basketball family was gravely ill. I told him how avidly Ruth followed his team and how sick she was. I asked him to contact her.

A few days later, a handwritten letter from Dean Smith arrived in Ruth's mail. Coach Smith told her how concerned he was for her health and how he hoped treatment would make her better. Then, he chatted about the next year's team and promised her that she'd be proud of them. Ruth was ecstatic. It was an act of grace and partnership for a prominent coach to write a dying fan.

Ruth succumbed to her cancer around Labor Day of that year. Her beloved Tarheels won the National Collegiate Basketball Championship the next spring. I'll bet she cheered from a blue heaven. I know I'll remain grateful to a celebrity who lived out an attitude of partnership.

Do you know the story of the Fisher King? It's another tale of partnership amid service. The story begins with the king as a boy who had gone into the forest to spend the night alone. This act would prove his courage and his fitness to serve as king. During the night, the king-to-be had a sacred vision. Out of the sacred fire appeared the Holy Grail, the symbol of God's divine grace. A voice announced, "You shall be keeper of the Grail, so that it may heal the hearts of men." But the boy became blinded by possibilities of power and glory. In a state of amazed ambition, he felt invincible and godlike. He grasped for the Grail through the fire, but the Grail vanished, leaving the king-to-be with a wounded hand.

As the boy grew into a king, his wound became even deeper. He searched for the Grail every day, but to no avail. Eventually his life lost its purpose. No one could reach him or help him. He lost faith in everyone, including himself. He could not love or feel love. His spirit began to die.

One day when the king had sunk into despair, a fool wandered into the castle and found him alone. Since the fool was simple-minded, he saw no king. He only saw a lonely man in terrible pain. The fool asked the monarch, "What ails you, friend?" "I need some water to cool my throat," replied the king.

The fool took a cup from the king's bedside table, filled it with water, and handed it to him. As the king began to drink, his wounds began to heal, and the cup magically became the Grail. The king turned to the fool in surprise and questioned, "How could you find that which my brightest and bravest could not? How did you know how to heal me and produce the Grail?" The fool replied, "I only knew that you were thirsty." Service meets simple needs, and miracles are the complicated by-products. Partnership and service go hand in hand.

How can we demonstrate an attitude of partnership? How do we live out partnerships of service? Ernest Mosley suggests how we can lead with a towel. We lead with a towel when we

> wipe the dirt from feet—
> with a word of encouragement
> or an expression of genuine concern.
> wipe the tears from others' eyes—
> by being sensitive to others' disappointments,
> losses, and sorrows.
> wipe the tears from others' faces—
> through restoring persons after failures,
> humiliations, or mistakes.
> wipe away the temptation to throw in the towel—
> in the face of personal and professional
> disappointments and obstacles in leadership.[2]

A STEWARDSHIP ATTITUDE

Leaders give what they have to their followers. Jesus, of course, gave the most. He gave his life as a ransom for many (Mark 10:45). We too become stewards in order to serve well. Unfortunately, we're not always clear about our own motives.

Jesus' most disquieting parable for me is the story of the sheep and goat judgment in Matthew 25. What surprises me is that both the blessed sheep and the cursed goats were startled. Apparently, neither knew how they had been blessed or cursed. Their spontaneous attitudes shaped their service . . . and sealed their fates.

"When the Son of Man comes in his glory, and all the angels with him, he will sit on his throne in heavenly glory. All the nations will be gathered before him, and he will separate the people one from another as a shepherd separates the sheep from the goats. He will put the sheep on his right and the goats on his left.

"Then the King will say to those on his right, 'Come, you who are blessed by my Father; take your inheritance, the kingdom prepared for you since the creation of the world. For I was hungry and you gave me something to eat, I was thirsty and you gave me something to drink, I was a stranger and you invited me in. I needed clothes and you clothed me. I was sick and you looked after me, I was in prison and you came to visit me.'

"Then the righteous will answer him, 'Lord, when did we see you hungry and feed you, or thirsty and give you something to drink? When did we see you a stranger and invite you in, or needing clothes and clothe you? When did we see you sick or in prison and go to visit you?'

"The King will reply, 'I tell you the truth, whatever you did for one of the least of these brothers of mine, you did for me.' " (Matthew 25:31-40)

Servant ministry—when it becomes ingrained in our basic identities—becomes a natural outgrowth of who we are. We do what we are. Service brings unexpected rewards. Failure to serve others becomes a surprising ground for judgment.

Our loves define us. Love gives what it has to give. Love doesn't require fame, fortune, or education. Love is simply a steward of itself. A few years ago I learned this lesson, up close and personal.

During the summer 1992, I discovered my brother, Jim, was suffering from the onset of leukemia. A bone marrow transplant was his only hope for life. My marrow was a perfect match, so off we went to the Hutchinson Cancer Center in Seattle, Washington. Neither of us knew what we were facing, but we both knew what we had to do.

For nearly a month, Jim and I underwent a rigorous preparation process. We both gave our medical histories, signed consent forms, attended the mandatory "some get well and some die" lectures, endured insurance negotiations, took numerous X-rays, and were introduced to support groups—a whirlwind of appointments and checkups that blurred together. Additionally, I banked blood in case I needed transfusions after the marrow harvest.

On October 29, Jim began a dozen days of high-dose chemotherapy and total body radiation. At last I understood fully how marrow transplants really work—the recipient is deliberately pushed to the brink of death and then rescued by implanting a new immune system. It was a brutal process to watch, and there was little I could do but watch and wait. The wait was excruciating. I began to fret. What if something goes wrong? What if I catch a bug? I found I would be harvested anyway. We had passed the point of no return. It was a tense process, and I was tension-filled.

Then transplant day arrived. On the morning of November 10, I awoke to find that I had relaxed. The marrow harvest was scheduled for 7:00 A.M., and I found I was ready. A subtle but important change had occurred in my attitude. Earlier, I had considered myself a donor. After all, that's what they had been calling me at the hospital. Somehow that signified to me that I had something the surgeons were going to take away. Before dawn on that Day Zero morning, I decided I had a gift to give and nobody had to take it from me.

This small difference in outlook made a huge difference in outcome for me. I was relaxed on the gurney outside the operating room—relaxed enough that the medical staff commented on how at ease I was. My harvest took only a bit over half of the usual length of time, especially surprising considering that my brother needed a full liter of marrow or roughly 5 percent of my supply. I didn't bleed, even after two hundred punctures of my pelvis. I woke up early with a clear head and lots of questions—so many that my recovery room nurse left me for other, needier patients, ones with less to talk about. Admittedly, for about a week, I did walk stiffly like Walter Brennan from the old *Real McCoys* TV series! But the process wasn't nearly as traumatic as I had feared.

My harvested marrow was strained to remove any bone chips and over a six-hour period dripped directly into my brother's bloodstream through a port in his chest. Jim had two birthdays that week—one on the tenth marking the beginning of a new life cycle, the other on the twelfth celebrating the beginning of his forty-eighth year of life. Balloons on his marrow bag and ribbon streamers on his bed told everyone that we had things to commemorate.

Then the waiting commenced again. This time we waited to see if the transplant would take. It was an excruciating few days. Platelets boosted the clotting abilities of Jim's fledgling blood system. Every day we waited for the blood counts to be recorded, hoping against hope for signs of a new immune system. But the counts didn't come, and Jim stayed very sick. Mouth sores left him unable to speak or swallow. His skin blistered. His mucous membranes exploded. He had to sleep on an air mattress—a surface that circulated air around his skin to help deal with bed sores. His face was puffy and discolored—as if he had fought the heavyweight champion of the world and lost. All of these phenomena were reportedly normal—but at this stage of healing, normal isn't good enough. You want to be well ahead of schedule.

Nearly two weeks into the waiting period after the transplant, disaster almost struck from a source I'd never anticipated. In the middle of the fourteenth night, Jim experienced "ICU psychosis." This phenomenon was the result of a month of extreme illness, powerful medicines, and long-term isolation. So, amid this confusion, Jim pulled all of his tubes out and nearly bled to death. The hospital staff handled this crisis calmly and professionally.

But, thereafter, a nurse sat in a rocker in the hall so that Jim was constantly in view.

Ironically, the morning following this near-miss, the blood counts blossomed. We had a graft! We had a chance! Jim exchanged his morphine pump for a breakfast menu—a surefire signal that he was on the mend. Other challenges, of course, occurred over time. But, we were on the way.

Jim remained in Seattle for another four months of treatments to fight off the setbacks that are common in the aftermath of transplants. I returned to Virginia. My friends and acquaintances questioned me about my experiences in Seattle. Many of them commented on how much courage I had shown. Even when I admitted how terrified I had been for Jim and me during much of my time in Seattle, some of these friends insisted on seeing the transplant as an act of courage. They were wrong. My donation of bone marrow was an act of love, a straightforward act of stewardship and servanthood.

The first evening I was in Seattle to begin the transplant process, Jim gave me a symbol and told me a story. The symbol was a lapel pin that said "110 %". That's what we were ready to give. I wore that pin every day in Seattle, and it rests on my desk now. The story came from Southwestern lore, from his experience in teaching on a Navajo reservation in Arizona. The Navajo language has no word for "thank you." They simply say, "You'd do the same for me."

(Jim used lots of homey sayings—sometimes seriously, often with tongue-in-cheek. When he needed to prove a point, he would simply declare his conclusion as "the Code of the West!" As it turned out, Jim humorously considered many things "the Code of the West." Now, you may understand better the dedication page for this book.)

Stewards give 110 percent. They give what they have out of love because—if the roles were reversed—the other person would likely offer the same gift. Love just gives whatever it has, whenever it can, and as freely as it can. That's the attitude effective leaders practice too.

UNSCIENTIFIC CONCLUSION

Our stance toward leadership isn't a scientific matter. Attitude, after all, is tough to weigh and measure. But, scientific or not, a servant attitude provides a strong and stable foundation for Christian leadership.

Lordship, partnership, and stewardship—these attitudes will serve Christian leaders well during the Information Age.

CHAPTER 4

Versatility: Broadening Meaning Through Leader Styles

Versatility is a requirement for effective leader style applications in this Information Age. Too often, Industrial Age leaders thought style—singular; Information Age leaders now think styles—plural. In the machine-minded Industrial Age, modern leaders thought and acted with an either-or, single best, one-size-fits-all mind-set toward leader style. But amid the multiplied challenges of an increasingly pluralistic era, interactive leaders are looking for both-and solutions. Deftness and versatility are part of the contemporary leader's job description.

AMBIDEXTROUS LEADERS

The emerging church needs flexible, adaptable, many-sided, multifaceted, inventive leaders. That's versatility—the capability of dealing with leadership dilemmas inventively. In fact, we need ambidextrous leaders today. These adept leaders are able and willing to approach opportunities from at least two sides. Ambidextrous leaders will become our meaning makers.

A high school friend of mine had the unusual ability of using both hands equally well. Jim wrote and ate left-handed. He threw and batted right-handed. Is it any wonder that he grew up to be an orthopedic surgeon who does surgery with either hand? He claims this trait has served him well in the operating room, because some surgical repairs must be made from awkward angles—if the surgeon is only able to use one hand in his or her work.

Ambidexterity is an apt metaphor for leaders in a connective era. *Ambi-*, the prefix meaning "both," hints at adroitness, at mastery from at least two points of view or with a minimum of two angles of attack. In a world of information glut, overchoice, and soaring expectations of churches, leaders who can marshal a range of resources and skills hold an obvious advantage over their one-dimensional sisters and brothers. Versatility comes with the leadership territory in our postmodern setting.

TWO ANGLES FOR LEADERSHIP

Switch-hitters in baseball have capitalized on their versatility by developing the ability to hit pitches from either side of the plate. Consequently, they always have the advantage of seeing curving pitches breaking in toward them, the best visual perspective for batters. Even when surprised by a pitch with an unexpected break or with unusual speed, switch-hitting batters still see the pitch better and increase their odds of hitting it solidly. In the same manner, interactive leaders cultivate the knack for seeing our world from angles that provide the optimum vantage point. We are, then, less likely to be handcuffed by circumstances.

Versatility is basic for effective leaders. But versatility can't become simply random and unintentional. If random, versatility can become completely arbitrary and lose its moorings. In other words, versatility requires a framework. Mission and morale provide that framework.

M & MS—NOT JUST CANDY ANYMORE

For me, leaders deal with two organizational dynamics constantly. Mission and morale—"the M & M factors"—are the baseline issues leaders must diagnose and balance every moment of their group lives. In fact, the classic studies of leadership usually broke leadership down into a dual watershed—a task-related aspect and a relational element. However these foundational ingredients of the leadership situation are described, they must be dealt with in ambidextrous fashion. Otherwise, the organization becomes lopsided, loses its balance, sacrifices its elasticity to the demands of change, and becomes unhealthy.

Meaning making, as a leadership art, grows out of mission and morale. The twin concerns of calling and community stretch today's leaders toward versatility automatically. When leaders help their groups clarify mission, they help others discover a meaningful calling—and then help their groups practice calling-in-community. When leaders help their groups raise morale, they help others belong to a meaningful community—and then help their groups become a community-of-calling.

Notice that leaders spotlight mission *and* morale, not mission or morale. Both concerns are always in the picture. That's not to say that mission and morale are present in exact balance in leaders. In reality, we are usually more comfortable and gifted in one area than the other. But leaders are responsible for assuring balanced or blended emphasis on mission and morale within the organization. On the other hand, mission and morale are rarely needed in equal amounts at any given point in an organization's life cycle. While one issue may be the focus of the viewfinder for a time, the other element must have its time in the picture or there's a price to be paid. Meaning making happens best when mission and morale are blended and balanced.

MISSION—WHAT TO DO?

Mission—variously called vision, tasks, goals, direction, dreams, external outcomes, market niches, calling, congregational personality—answers the basic question, What will we do?[1] Wider-then-narrower is the theme of mission-oriented groups.

Mission-tilted leaders frequently target growth and change issues—new members, new converts, new church starts.

Activist congregations frequently fall into a mission-first-last-and-always perspective of church life. These mission-centered perspectives get results quickly but may underestimate the importance of morale issues in the health of the church. While productive when measured solely by efficiency, the blind spot of these task-oriented groups may open their doors to conflict and even schism.

In the words of a megachurch pastor, "I had to run off seven hundred members to save this church!" Personally, I don't know what issues were at stake in that particular case. But I hear group mission being emphasized—even at the risk of congregational morale. Versatility is sacrificed when leaders make "my way or the highway" the only options for followers.

MORALE—CAN DO!

Morale—sometimes referred to as *esprit de corps,* the spirit of the group, fellowship, internal care, congregational well-being—makes the basic affirmation, We can do it![2] Wider-then-deeper is the intention of morale-centered groups. Morale is fuel for action. Morale-tilted leaders often spend energy on belonging, inclusion, mediation of differences and conflicts, personal development, and community enrichment.

Atmosphere-oriented congregations major on fellowship and may minor on progress. "Peace at any price," "Don't rock the boat," or "Just keep the troops happy" make morale the highest leadership value. Productivity or efficiency is not apt to be leaders' interest, making them vulnerable to the complaints of their mission-attentive members. If "feel good" faith becomes the norm for a congregation, the balance between mission and morale may be sacrificed.

M & M COMPARED AND CONTRASTED

Mission and morale are two sides of the coin in effective leadership. (Remember that effectiveness—doing the right thing—is poles apart from efficiency—doing things right.) Leaders both clarify mission *and* heighten morale. Consequently, healthy congregations have a sharp sense of their direction and a high sense of their ability to act successfully.

Note the comparisons and contrasts between mission and morale below. Pay special attention to the morale side of the equation. The morale column is apt to challenge religious leaders the most. Why? Because much of the art and science of leadership came into formal ministerial training from more mission-oriented business and military sources. However, even these disciplines are increasingly recognizing that groups crave balance in mission and morale, especially in volunteer groups.

MISSION	*MORALE*
"Doing"	"Being"
Skill	Will
Goals	Goodwill
Targets	Teamwork
Stability	Loyalty
Planned Change	Stability Zones
Task-orientation	Relational-orientation
High Structure	Low Anxiety
Tradition	Trust
Commitment	Confidence
Action	Attitude

Imbalance has some religious predicators. For example, congregations and denominations on the extremes of the theological spectrum are generally more likely to emphasize a focused agenda, a structured mission. In broad terms, more mainstream congregations and denominations tend to stress supportive or morale-centered issues. Both patterns have built-in imbalance and call for leaders who can help the group deal with the risks of preferring mission over morale, or morale over mission.

VERSATILITY—A PATCHWORK QUILT OF DYNAMICS AND ROLES

Let's take the basic leadership dynamics of mission and morale and create a patchwork quilt for the practice of leadership by interlacing the fundamental roles of community builder, group anchor, and team orienteer. These six interactions become blocks for the quilt of leadership versatility.

	Missions <——> Morale
Community Builder	TEAMWORK <——> TRUST
Group Anchor	MODELING <——> MARVELING
Team Orienteer	NAVAGATION <——> NERVE

Let's trace the mission-and-morale theme through the early section of Mark's Gospel as an example of stitching together our leadership quilt. Think of Mark 3–6 as a case study in leadership versatility.

First, mission and morale interact in the leader's community-building role as teamwork and trust. In Mark 3:13-15, Jesus sets out a mission to preach and to have authority to drive out demons (Mark 3:14-15), calling for teamwork. On the morale side of the community-building equation, trust is evident in his desire for the disciples to be with him (Mark 3:14).

Second, mission and morale emerge also as leaders function as group anchors. In Mark 4:35-41, Jesus stilled the storm. He modeled a stable focus that amazed his disciples. As a result, they both explored who Jesus was and, on a more mundane level, safely crossed the Sea of Galilee (Mark 5:1). From a morale standpoint, they moved from panic in the face of the gale to marveling at a leader who could deal serenely with their terror (Mark 4:39-41).

Third, mission and morale blend into the leader's team orienteering role as navigation and nerve. In Mark 6, Jesus sent out the seventy with a clear mandate and instructions to travel light (Mark 6:8-11); they had their navigational charts. Simultaneously, the disciples had the nerve to undertake exactly what they had been directed to do (Mark 6:12-13, 30).

EXPANDING YOUR COMFORT ZONE

Can you succeed as a meaning-making leader in the Information Age? The secret can now be told. Your leadership versatility is enlarged by or limited by your personal comfort zone. You will succeed or fail based on whether or not you can expand your personal and professional comfort zone.

Your comfort zone builds on behaviors that are easily within your reach. Unfortunately, your comfort zone, your relaxed and assured range of leadership behaviors, often becomes an either-or proposition. It either opens many potential possibilities or puts the brakes on your ability to meet novelty flexibly.

At least four ingredients define your comfort zone. Habits, models, skills, and beliefs can bless or curse you as a leader.

1. Habits grow out of what we've seen and, consequently, what we've done. They become routine or, worse yet, become ruts that blindfold us. The warning written on the banners at the western end of St. Joseph, Missouri's Main Street during the days of the wagon trains applies to contemporary leaders' habits too: "Choose your rut carefully. You may be in it all the way to California!"

2. Models—those persons whose leadership we have personally seen and admired—can limit us unconsciously to their abilities and opportunities, not ours. We may adopt our models' comfort zones, and never realize it. Psychologists claim we usually mimic our heroes' and heroines' weak points, not their strengths. Why? Because we see tangibles and imitate them but are blind to intangibles and ignore them.

3. Our skill set, if wide and rich, can create leadership options for us. Or, if our skills are narrow and restricted, we can remain uncomfortable with new situations. Remember the old joke about the gorilla who played golf? His owner got him

into a (somewhat skeptical) foursome at the country club for a friendly game one Saturday morning. The three human partners were more than a little curious about the gorilla's golfing skills. On the first tee, the gorilla took a driver and muscled the ball onto the green, four hundred yards away! The other golfers could hardly believe their eyes. They had never seen a golf ball hit so far and so straight. On the green, the gorilla lined up his putt, took his driver, and drove the ball another four hundred yards! His comfort zone only included one club in his bag.

Onesidedness kills versatility. Distance was the gorilla's forte, and finesse was his weakness. If the golfing axiom "drive for show—putt for dough" is correct, this gorilla was doomed to poverty! So is any leader who has a skill range that's too narrow for his or her situational demands. Versatility requires that Information Age leaders must play every club in their bags.

4. Beliefs restrict leaders' comfort zones too. Many of us hold some views—theological, cultural, or psychological—so ardently that we discount other perspectives automatically. We are averse to or afraid of possibilities that run counter to our point of view. As a result, any behavior that is antithetical to what a leader believes in, something that goes against his or her principles, is not something the person is likely to adopt.[3] As hard as it is for religious leaders to admit, our beliefs both define and blind us. No wonder Jesus dared his followers to develop seeing eyes and hearing ears.

Actually, your comfort zone is elastic. In reality, you have access to at least part of your leadership resource inventory most of the time. When all the best features of your habits, models, skills, and beliefs are usable in leadership, you're in your "comfort zone." When you can retrieve and use most of your resources, you're in your "support zone." When only some of your resources are available, you're in your "stretch zone." When few or none of your leader resources are accessible or relevant, you're in your "discomfort zone." The goal is to stay in your comfort zone much of the time, use your support and stretch zones as needed, and avoid your discomfort zone as much as possible.

So how can you become a better steward of your comfort zone and use your support, stretch, and discomfort zones appropriately? Know them. Challenge them. Stretch them. How? We know our comfort zone better when we ask those who know us best to help us evaluate our strengths and weaknesses. Supervisors, support groups, family, and instruments help us explore our comfort and other zones of functioning. We challenge our comfort zones when we learn new information and look at the world through larger frameworks. We stretch our comfort zones when we recruit mentors, coaches, therapists, and consultants to guide us in self-awareness and self-development for leadership.

PRINCIPLES OF VERSATILITY[4]

In the days of the ancient mariners, maps and navigational charts were either nonexistent or notoriously inaccurate. Consequently, navigators and sea captains kept narratives—called rutters[5]—to guide them on return trips. The specific course between where we are as leaders and where we want to go requires precision, the kind of exactness that comes from advance scouts who have already made the voyage. These guidelines provide us a wider view of our leadership practices. These principles help us balance mission and morale for greater versatility.

1. Mission and morale are both necessities for congregational health. Versatile leaders school themselves in moving easily across the mission-morale continuum.

2. Mission and morale are needed in blends and with balance for congregational effectiveness. Otherwise, either mission or morale suffers.

3. Most leaders and congregations are lopsided or "M & M disadvantaged." Personal or organizational excellence in either mission or morale may create a comfort zone or even a dependence that undercuts the "off suit." Or, to state this theme

differently, any strength—when overused—becomes a weakness. Paradoxically, even our leader strengths can snuff out our versatility and, therefore, our effectiveness.

4. There is a faith component in our M & M mix. Leadership is theological as well as pragmatic. Ironically, when leaders have a passionate conviction that guides should be either tough (mission-oriented) or tender (morale-oriented), they exclude the opposite preference and its set of behaviors.

If one perspective is "good," the opposite option is assumed to be "bad" or even sinful. What we believe, the inner aspect of leadership, polarizes our ability to act flexibly. To revisit our architectural model of leadership, stance shapes style, and attitude is the foundation for action.

5. To expand our versatility as leaders, we have two basic challenges. We have both to expand our skill repertoire and to change our beliefs about leadership and followership. The first challenge is much easier than the second. Changing our skill set is always easier than changing our mind.

6. Realistic and accurate evaluation of our mission and morale mix provides the basis for growth in style versatility. Knowing how we mix mission and morale maps our strengths and weaknesses.

7. We should prize and use our strengths—in the process of monitoring performance and results—to see if our blind spots are sabotaging us. Effective leaders must forever and always be committed to self-awareness. After all, our best gifts to the world as leaders are our best selves, disciplined under God, and offered for the health of our group.

8. De-emphasize overdeveloped and overused elements. Moderating overused strengths lessens our overdependence on these elements. Rheostating an overused strength dims its glare but doesn't turn off its light.

9. Stretch to develop and use any underemployed style elements. It's natural to ignore underused abilities—that's how they remain underdeveloped. When areas of underuse are pinpointed, steps can be deliberately taken to stretch our

behavioral range. We may challenge ourselves to grow and increase our style array. We may build a balanced team of coministers and delegate. Or we may choose to use gadgets and tools, computerized and otherwise, to fill gaps.

10. Time the use of strengths. Pacing and timing are crucial aspects of the artistry of leadership. Become a steward of when to apply the mission-morale mix to your own leadership opportunities.

11. Juggle leadership's roles deliberately. When we function as team orienteers, we are emphasizing the mission side of the leadership ledger. When we function as community builders, we are spotlighting the morale dimension of leadership. When we function as group anchors, we are stressing the bridge or modeling aspect of leadership.

MISSION <——> MORALE
MODELING

As models, we personalize our leadership beliefs and practices. We embody and act out the meaning-making process as we blend and balance mission and morale.

MISSION AND MORALE'S TEST PATTERNS

Since we are leaders who operate from a belief system, we learn quickly to test the patterns of our versatility from a theological perspective. Again, let's apply a block of Scripture to our leadership practice for clues and cues. Using a middle section of Luke's Gospel, at least four theological tests emerge from Jesus' leadership approach.

First, are we versatile enough to carry the fallen ones (Luke 5:17-26)? Early in Jesus' ministry, people flocked to watch the unfolding of works of healing and forgiveness. One of the best-known of these events was the healing of the man who was paralyzed who had to be lowered through the roof. Not only was the friends' mission of physical and spiritual wholeness achieved, their morale soared, leaving them awed, amazed, praising God, and aware that they had seen remarkable things that day (Luke 5:26).

Second, are we versatile enough to welcome the little ones (Luke 9:46-48)? From the beginning, the kingdom of God was difficult for Jesus' apprentices to grasp. Repeatedly, they struggled with who was greatest in God's kingdom. On this occasion, Jesus illustrated greatness by having a small child stand beside him and by speaking about hospitality. "Whoever welcomes this little child in my name welcomes me; and whoever welcomes me welcomes the one who sent me. For he who is least among you all—he is the greatest" (Luke 9:48). After all, mission and morale in leadership blend attitude with action.

Third, are we versatile enough to restore the beaten ones (Luke 10:30-37)? How do we react to situations of human brokenness? Is our mission broad enough and flexible enough to meet needs on the periphery of our personal and professional pilgrimage? Can we provide support for others in ways that lift their morale? The story of the good Samaritan raises these and other questions for sensitive leaders.

Fourth, are we versatile enough to straighten the bent ones (Luke 13:10-13)? Jesus saw clearly that the Sabbath and its activities are designed to help persons crippled by evil to walk tall again. In this case, a woman who had been crippled by a spirit for eighteen years (Luke 13:11) was freed from her infirmity and responded with health and joy, a clear mix of mission and morale.

THE DARK SIDE OF ACTIVISM

A guide's style of leadership is, by definition, operational. Leader style is demonstrated every day in the way the facilitator acts. Even in an Information Age when meaning making is the paramount leadership responsibility, action is still the primary indicator of style patterns. But for some religious leaders, activity and action can become a blind spot.

Why can activity become a trap for Western leaders? Observers have noted that American religion is more pragmatic than reflective, more activistic than thoughtful. These two qualities create an exciting but risky mix for today's religious leaders in Western culture. Americans are activists. We have traditionally adopted an aggressive, frontier perspective on religious leadership. We push the envelope, do something new, do it now, and act with confidence and flair.

Conrad Cherry, of the Center for the Study of Religion and American Culture at Indiana University and Purdue University, Indianapolis, makes a telling observation about the faith style of Americans: "Americans have a tendency to take their religion straight . . . [we] don't water it down with a lot of intellectualism." [6] The danger of this approach to faith for leaders is simple—we may act for the sake of acting, even before we have established a foundation for acting. Like ships without rudders, we sail from storm to storm until we crash on the rocks.

When action becomes the only attribute of leadership, more thoughtful values suffer. Worse yet, facilitators may act without values. Rootless actors or reactors are dangerous leaders. They do things—lots of things—but lack a doctrinal foundation. The best of all the preachers are men who live by their creeds, claimed Edgar A. Guest. Versatility in leadership style that's anchored in the dynamics of mission and morale has a solid operational framework for leaders.

STYLE SMORGASBORD

Andy Warhol claimed that, sooner or later, everyone is famous for fifteen minutes. Apparently he overlooked James David Barber, who moves into the national spotlight at least every four years. Barber, a political scientist at Duke University and an active churchperson, has attracted media attention by predicting the future behaviors of presidential candidates. Barber's leadership clues emerge from the study of two qualities from leaders' pasts. First, Barber examines activity-passivity, or how much energy leaders invest in their roles. Second, Barber examines "positive-negative affect" or how leaders handle power. Taken together, these two dynamics reveal glimpses of character and either enhance or limit leaders' versatility.

Versatility needs an anchor in character to keep it from becoming random and rootless. Character—those patterns of everyday behavior flowing from our moral values—provides an important lens through which leadership versatility can be viewed. The Sermon on the Mount said it first: We are known by the fruits of our lives (Matthew 7:15-20). Leader style is, after all, the product of our behavioral patterns.

Character is an especially crucial component of leadership in churches, service, and volunteer organizations. Like political leaders, ministers deal constantly with emotional issues and changing constituencies. If pastors lose credibility and trust, their volunteers take their energies to other causes and leave the former guide marching alone at the head of a follower-free column. Barber's two dynamics of character yield a smorgasbord of four distinct styles of leadership. Like all leader styles, each individual approach has some advantages as well as containing the seeds of its own destruction. These four styles illustrate the range of versatile behavior patterns available to those who would lead others.

Catalytic Blends of Mission and Morale

Active-passive leaders, or catalysts, balance mission and morale creatively and are typically at ease with themselves and with power. They usually work energetically, productively, and joyfully. Most catalysts think on their feet well and relate flexibly. Their Achilles' heel is others' rigidity and irrationality. They assume a fairly sane world, and when they encounter craziness, they may lose effectiveness as they wonder how others can veer so far off course.

Commanding Blends of Mission and Morale

Active-negative leaders, or commanders, emphasize mission over morale and are typically narrowly focused strivers. They often see life as a struggle and plunge in aggressively. Commanders appear to be trying to make up for something and suffer at times from perfectionism. Their weakness is an overemphasis on mission and power; active-negative leaders frequently become overcontrolling and judge others harshly.

Encouraging Blends of Mission and Morale

Passive-active leaders, or encouragers, stress morale over mission and take their cues from others in approval-seeking behaviors. They tend to be agreeable, cooperative, and hopeful. The dark side of passive-active leaders is that their need to be liked leaves them dependent on their followers and may call on them to spend their energies in short-term initiatives.

Hermit Blends of Mission and Morale

Passive-negative leaders, or hermits, emphasize neither mission nor morale. These persons take a "have to" stance toward responsibility. They prefer to stand back, go by the book, and expect others to do things decently and in order too. Unable to invest energy in relationships or to appreciate the realities of power, hermits often follow their followers in the final analysis.

VERSATILITY—LATITUDE AND LIMITS

Every leadership style has some predictability, and, therefore, its own latitude in and limits on versatility. Catalyst leaders aim for balanced results and develop the next generation of leaders. Commander leaders pursue power and keep it, leaving their followers unable to grow into leaders. Encouragers are thirsty for love, neglecting the longer-term health of their organizations. Hermits are driven by personal survival. Each style selection has its own patterns and restrictions on versatility.

WANTED: VERSATILE LEADERS

"Little-Johnny-one-note" leaders are dinosaurs in today's world. A connective, interactive, systemic, webbed world demands flexibility, a rich skill array, and versatility. Leaders who aren't ready to pay the price of self-evaluation and self-growth must get ready for Jurassic Park.

CHAPTER 5

Vision: Focusing Meaning Through Leader Strategies

Targeted action is a necessity for leaders. Focus allows leaders to act selectively and strategically. Since no leader can be in two places at once or spend a day or a dollar two different ways, strategic focus is fundamental to effective leaders.

Focus gives leaders a track to run on. Focus steadies us when we are buffeted, grounds us when we're distracted, and homes us in when we've wandered off course. Focus lends perspective by making big issues even larger and by reducing minor matters to even smaller scope. You and I can see how focused Jesus was just by observing when and why he chose to pull back for perspective on his ministry.[1] He withdrew for personal renewal, prayer, and decision making (Mark 1:35; Luke 6:12). He drew back when he was in danger of being mistaken merely for a healer or a fast-food supplier (Mark 1:45; John 6:15). He moved on when there were other places to preach (Luke 4:43). He retreated when he had gone as far as he could against opposition (Mark 3:7). These and other strategic retreats allowed Jesus to stay sharply focused on his unique mission.

THE FEW, THE PROUD, THE BRAVE

Imagine this true-life situation. You're walking down a real street in Kokomo, Indiana, and you read this actual sign: "Burgers,

Fries, Shakes, Bait." Would you likely drop in for a meal there? Would you consider any store where menu options might include "a cheeseburger with a side order of night crawlers" to have lost its strategic focus? I would!

When organizations, including churches, try to be and to do everything for everybody all at once, they make a common discovery. They are aiming at too many targets simultaneously and, consequently, are apt to miss the bull's-eye on all of them. Seasoned wildfowl hunters—especially quail hunters—know that the dumb luck approach of firing randomly into a covey usually isn't the best way to put roast quail on the dinner table. The best hunters select one bird in the larger covey and aim only for it. They use a targeted philosophy—literally.

Try to put yourself into the boots of a quail hunter. Think strategically about your experience. First, you flush the birds out of hiding. If you don't know where the birds are, the hubbub of the covey taking flight startles you momentarily. If you do know where the birds are, the speed and sound of quail taking flight is still a bit disorienting. You choose one bird in the covey, aim, lead the bird, and fire. Hear the focus inherent to the strategic process? You master your emotions. You act selectively. You fire not where the bird is, but where the bird will be. Remember the formula for athletic success offered by Wayne Gretzky, the best hockey player of all time? He claimed, "I skate to where the puck will be, not where it was." That's strategic thinking and acting. This feel for anticipation lays the foundation for effective strategic leadership.

CHOOSING WHO WE WILL BE

Anticipation applies to organizational strategies too. Some marketing strategists claim organizations have basically only three options. Therefore, they must anticipate and choose a primary focus from these foundational alternatives in order to succeed. According to this approach, an organization can either be the first, the finest, or the friendliest.[2] The core alternatives are simple. A group can become the earliest to offer a service or product—a traditional edge for Old Firsts or for innovative congregations. Or, a group can provide the highest quality ministries, services, or products—an advantage for congregations whose emphasis on "the best" appeals to the style of members as well as on the substance of the ministry. Or a group can create the closest customer intimacy—a strategic strength for congregations who pursue warm relationships through fellowship or morale issues. The trick is to choose to be first or finest or friendliest and to major on that choice zealously—with never more than a minor interest in any secondary option. The strategic agenda can't become cluttered without undercutting a congregation's ministry focus and its odds of succeeding in its work.

It is not just a matter of choosing your battles carefully and counting the cost to keep from losing. To state the issue much more positively, by picking our battles selectively, we also hope to secure our victories. We're investing our lives in our preferred futures. That's thinking and acting strategically.

MEASURING TWICE, CUTTING ONCE

When leaders begin to think and act strategically, we match our future targets and our present resources carefully and deliberately. Norm Abram, the master carpenter who hosts "The New Yankee Workshop" and cohosts the popular home renovation series, *This Old House,* on public television, has written a charming little book on strategy. Concentrating on the craft of selecting tools for woodworking, Abram counsels artisans to *Measure Twice, Cut Once.*[3] That title shouts "strategy," doesn't it? In other words, strategists reflect before we act. We deliberately make choices and then target our tailored behaviors to those decisions. When we deliberately select possibilities, visualize outcomes, plan for goals, and apply our resources to our primary tasks, we are thinking and acting strategically.

FINDING AND EXTENDING OUR "EDGE"

Strategy is the art of "edge finding" and "edge extending."[4] In ministry, leaders first find what their congregation does best—its edge—and then help that congregation do its best even better. Such guides help their organizations frame their mission and values in ways that "members find transcendent."[5] Simply put, strategy is the stewardship of strengths. Strategy, for churches and ministers, happens at the intersections of our strengths and others' needs. Edges, or advantages, are enriched and extended so that our best ministry resources are used intentionally on our best ministry opportunities.

Norm Abram mastered carpentry under his father's tutelage. It's a common pattern for artisans.[6] Crafts often are learned in an apprentice-mentor relationship. In fact, Jesus may have honed the arts of strategy in Joseph's carpentry shop. The process of creation, whether it's applied to furniture or to congregational futures, calls for strategic artistry. To excel in this most cerebral of the leader's arts—strategy—requires seasoned coaching in strategy.

THE NEW TESTAMENT AS
A STRATEGY MENTOR

Christians have a ready resource in strategic thinking and acting, the New Testament itself. The sweeping saga of leadership in the New Testament serves as a sage tutor in the arts of strategic ministry. In fact, a crisp strategic cycle or pattern emerges clearly from the pages of the Christian story. This New Testament pattern of strategy is threefold—with a fourth element reserved for unique crises. Strategy begins with and builds on a foundation of focus. Then, new opportunities to apply the strategic focus require flexibility. Next, as focusing with flexibility succeeds and becomes successfully established, the challenge of remaining future-oriented arises. That's the basic New Testament pattern of strategy—focus, flexibility, and future-orientation.[7]

THE "GENERATIONS" OF STRATEGY

JESUS	ACTS	PASTORALS	REVELATION
FIRST	SECOND	THIRD	FOURTH
LAUNCH	EXPAND	ESTABLISH	SURVIVE
FOCUS	FLEXIBILITY	FUTURE	FEASIBILITY

That's the basic strategy cycle until a traumatic crisis confronts the church. Then an additional element is added temporarily. When calamity occurs, feasibility also becomes a strategic issue. That is, when our lives fall down around our ears, we do what we can feasibly do with integrity in order to survive. The intent, of course, is to return as soon as we can to the basic threefold strategic cycle of (1) focusing (2) with flexibility (3) on the future.

FOCUSING ON A TARGET

Jesus was a supremely focused leader, a strategic leader at every point of his ministry. He had a sense of transcendent purpose.[8] Jesus obviously had a sense of calling and personal focus early in his life. For example, at age twelve in the Temple, he declared that he "must be in my Father's house" (Luke 2:49). However, from age twelve to about thirty, the New Testament doesn't record Jesus' specific thoughts or actions. What happened during the eighteen silent years in Jesus' life? Could anything strategic have been unfolding in his young years? Of course, it's only speculative, but I wonder if Jesus didn't sharpen his focus as a strategic leader in Joseph's carpentry shop.

Strategic thinking is an art and a craft, perhaps best learned from artisans and craftspersons like Joseph. Carpenters in biblical times were jacks-of-all-trades. Without standard measures, sophisticated tools, or lumber yards, carpenters were home and furniture designers, tool makers, and woodsmen and lumbermen. They crafted furnishings and structures from the first description of the item by the customer to the final use of the item. They visualized, planned, gathered raw materials, worked through the fit-and-finish process, and completed the product. The overall process of moving from emerging vision to practical outcome is the essence of strategy. If Jesus sharpened his self-definition for nearly two decades, it's no wonder Jesus launched his ministry with a clear focus, is it?

During the temptations, Jesus refused to be diverted from his calling and strategic mission. Three times the tempter attempted to get Jesus to do the right things by the wrong means. And, three times Jesus stayed on track to serve God as the inaugurator of the kingdom of God. That kind of constancy results from clarity of calling and mission.

KINGDOM DREAMS

The kingdom of God provided the visionary core of Jesus' life and work. His first recorded statement centered on the kingdom: "The time has come. The kingdom of God is near. Repent and believe the good news!" (Mark 1:15). More than one hundred times in the Gospels, Jesus announced and embodied his passion—the kingdom of God. He lived and died to introduce the world to God's reign over individual and corporate life. It was his consistent message.

The strategic themes of the kingdom of God are eternal.[9] They concern Jesus' gift of salvation, God's rule among people, and the necessity for change within believers.

1. The kingdom brings redemption to us. "Redemption"

describes the purpose of God in one word. Consequently, Jesus' parables speak of grace graphically in the two stories of two debtors (Luke 7:36-50); lost sheep, lost coin, and lost sons (Luke 15:1-32); and unforgiving debtors (Matthew 18:23-35).

2. The kingdom reminds us that God rules. Individuals and organizations thrive under God's reign. Believers are obedient to their king. God's will and regime are the core of the stories about tower builders and warring kings (Luke 14:28-33), hidden treasures and precious pearls (Matthew 13:44-46), unresponsive neighbors and callous judges (Luke 11:5-8; 18:2-8), and farmers and helpers (Luke 17:7-10).

3. The kingdom creates change. Growth is a constant in Jesus' stories about the kingdom. To encounter God is to be called to maturity like seeds growing secretly (Mark 4:26-29); mustard seeds and leaven (Luke 13:18-21; Mark 4:30-32); and kernels of wheat (John 12:24).

FAITHFUL FOLLOWERS

Interestingly, Jesus' followers also maintained his energy for the kingdom of God. Luke, writer of the only two-volume Gospel and history in the New Testament, spotlights the kingdom theme. At the beginning of his ministry in Luke, Jesus proclaims: "I must preach the good news of the kingdom of God . . . because that is why I was sent" (Luke 4:43). At the end of Acts, the second volume in this set, Paul has reached Rome and has witnessed there to the Jews and the Gentiles. Acts concludes with a note about God's kingdom: "Boldly and without hindrance he preached the kingdom of God and taught about the Lord Jesus Christ" (Acts 28:31).

Visionaries are rarely welcomed or understood. But every generation needs its dreamers. Unfortunately, idealists are seen most benignly as renegades, rebels, iconoclasts; more appreciatively as seers; prophets; and worst as troublemakers or heretics. What these constructive critics of the past and present give us is a glimpse of the future. Their strategic focus creates a telescope, a window on tomorrow so we can see what can be through a glass darkly at least.

AMPLIFYING SOULS

James Dickey, poet and author of the novel *Deliverance,* died while this book was being written. He liked to be pictured as a hard-drinking, high-living writer in the mold of Hemingway. Dickey could be difficult to relate to at times. He admitted he could be a jerk.

Dickey also liked variety in the topics, styles, and types of literature he produced. He readily and happily switched from poetry to fiction, always with conflict as the underlying issue. Basically, Dickey saw writing as wrestling meaning to the ground.

For thirty years James Dickey served as poet-in-residence at the University of South Carolina. In a 1990 English class, he suggested a single-minded, strategic focus for writers like himself. He proposed, "For everybody in this class I wish only one thing, that you concentrate your efforts to one end. Not to publish. Not to be famous. Not to make money. . . . Concentrate all your energies toward writing something that will stand up, that will move people, that will stay with them, disturb them, amplify . . . their souls."[10] Amplifying souls is as good a focus for congregational leaders as it is for writers.

FLEXIBILITY WITH FOCUS

The biblical story of Acts and the churches introduces us to the second and perhaps the trickiest element of strategy—flexibility. The trick for strategic leaders is to respond flexibly to new opportunities without sacrificing focus. Too often leaders lock into a strategic focus so totally that they are blind to fresh openings. Or they prize flexibility so much they become faddish and forget the basic vision. Either way, strategic ministry suffers.

The church leaders of Acts, mostly unknown and anonymous,

walked boldly and flexibly through God's new doors of mission and ministry. Yet, they stayed focused on establishing the kingdom of God. The Holy Spirit pointed the early church toward new, untried frontiers, and they seized the day for Christ. Focus with flexibility was their strategic style.

FLEXIBILITY FOR NEW CHALLENGES

Focus with flexibility is not easy for leaders to maintain. Take for example Thomas Edison's invention of the incandescent lightbulb. For fifty years electric lights, both arc and incandescent, had been experimented with in Europe and the United States.

In 1878 Edison was experiencing burnout. He needed a rest and perhaps a new challenge. He found both. Edison had been working tirelessly for seven years with the phonograph, his most noteworthy invention at that time. After a brief trip and change of pace, he was dazzled by a demonstration of arc lights in early September of 1878.

In a flash of intuition, Edison saw a bigger vision for electric lights than anyone before him had grasped. His goal was to put electric lights into every residence and to supply them by a network of electrical power akin to gas lines. Edison had a new strategic focus.

Edison and his team of inventors attacked this new challenge and turned the laboratory at Menlo Park into a beehive of creativity. Three large barriers had to be crossed for Edison's vision of an electrical distribution system for the masses to become a reality. Reliable, steady electric power supplies, conductors, and circuits had to be provided. Vacuums had to be developed in order for sealed, incandescent bulbs to be manufactured. And, finally, a durable filament had to be devised for the bulb.

Electrical supplies and vacuums proved to be the easier obstacles to conquer. But inventing a filament for the lightbulb remained elusive. Although financial backers had formed a new company called the Edison Electrical Light Company, their patience began to wane. They questioned Edison; his detractors spoke strongly against this unschooled mechanic. Edison's focus was being tested.

In spite of the scientific failures and bad publicity, Edison never lost heart or vision. He kept his focus and applied that focus with flexibility. He tried a variety of potential filament materials—platinum, carbon, boron, chromium, tungsten, and nickel. All failed. But Edison and his team persisted.

After hundreds of technical failures and fourteen months of intensive experimentation, Edison found the filament materials he had so desperately searched for—carbon scraped from blackened lamp globes molded to paper. Focus with flexibility had finally paid off. On November 1, 1879, Edison applied for a patent for a carbon filament lamp, the first practical and economical electric light for mass domestic use. That's what we remember Edison for. But his broader vision of the large-scale production, sale, and use of electric power soon followed and brought illumination to our world. Edison never wavered from his focused vision. And he remained flexible in his search for the practical inventions to make his dream come true.

FLEXIBILITY, FOCUS—BOTH/AND

Focus and flexibility frequently compete in tug-of-war fashion. During the Industrial Age, the motto of wing walkers made perfect sense: "Don't let go of what you've got hold of until you've gotten a good grip on something else." Why? Because the emphasis of the old paradigm was focus. But, in the Information Age, the only way to make progress is to let go of what you've got hold of and go for it. It's the only path to new experiences, the sole road to the future.[11] The opportunity of the emerging paradigm is to live flexibly while maintaining focus.

FUTURE IN THE FOREGROUND

When any church feels it has arrived, it takes on an establishment mind-set. The "establishment church" is convinced that it has a heritage worth protecting, and invests more emotionally in the past than the future. Since the Church is, by definition a conserving institution, it's too easy and too natural for congregations to adopt a backward direction. But preserving and conserving aren't the same as serving. "Establishment churches" subtly shift our energy from leading the movement to tending the monument—a risky, if not deadly, stewardship of energy. The tragic risk in protecting our past is that we may, in the process, forfeit our future.

The Pastoral Epistles of 1 and 2 Timothy and Titus demonstrate the tension between a past-orientation and a future-orientation in congregational life. By late in the first century, structured congregations had emerged out of the church's missionary efforts. The Pastorals, sometimes called the earliest pastor's handbooks in the New Testament, instruct ministers in how to lead established congregations. Practical suggestions are made on how to proclaim the gospel, to care for hurting and needy members, and to lead the congregation. Even at this early date in the Christian movement, the establishment perspective already had a firm toehold among the faithful.

But from the view of the future, the tone of the Pastorals is strikingly ominous. Read the text of these three books aloud and listen for negative, backward looking verbs. The mood is aimed toward the past, toward preserving what has been. For example, believers are counseled in holding on to faith (1 Timothy 1:19). Pastors and leaders are urged to guard the good deposit (2 Timothy 1:14); endure hardship (2 Timothy 2:3); correct, rebuke, encourage (2 Timothy 4:2-3); straighten out (Titus 1:5); hold firmly (Titus 1:9); and rebuke them sharply (Titus 1:13). The future fades quickly when more value is placed on the past. When bygone years dominate our thinking, we become staunch defenders of what has been and forfeit what is still to come. When God

91

is seen only as a traditionalist, leaders face the challenge of creating a healthier theology for themselves.

The standard time zone for the Pastoral Epistles is yesterday. That can be suicide, strategically speaking, for congregations. Targeted anticipation is the acid test for strategic leaders. Leaders are interested in the future for one simple reason—they expect to live the rest of their lives in the future. Congregations will live in the future too—if they choose it.

UNABLE TO SEIZE THE FUTURE

Sometimes we unintentionally position ourselves to win the past and lose the future. Let me give you an illustration from horticulture of the past-versus-future tension. The winter of 1996 was extremely severe for the Mid-Atlantic region. Many trees literally froze to death in this area. I lost an evergreen shrub from my front yard due to the icy weather.

Here's how and why the shrub died. In early February our area was hit by a heavy ice storm and sustained near-zero temperatures. Since Richmond, Virginia, is in a fairly temperate climate zone, our city workers were ill-equipped to conquer the snow-clogged streets. When the streets were finally plowed, large chunks of ice were strewn over the curbs and into yards. My front yard had a pile of icebergs about three feet deep all along the street side. As some thawing occurred, I noticed a strange sight. A small evergreen bush at the curb near my driveway had been completely rolled out of the earth by the force of the ice thrown up into my yard by the snowplows.

Closer examination of the shrub showed clearly why the plant had been turned upside down so easily. Although the evergreen had been in the earth for about fifteen years, it had never taken root. Why? Because this shrub, as an infant plant, had been left in a nursery's container too long. Its root system had grown in a tight circle within its container for so long that—even though the shrub had had more than a decade with plenty of room to expand and to put its roots deep in the soil—it had actually forgotten how to extend its roots. The root ball for this mature plant had remained only eight inches deep and the same width. The shrub's past had doomed its future. Then the weight of the ice, taken from the side of the plant, had been too much. The shrub's roots froze quickly and fatally in the exposure of subzero windchills.

Plants left too long in nursery containers develop a "container consciousness." The roots get into the habit of growing around and around inside the confines of the container. When these plants are transplanted, they continue to grow in the same familiar circles. The only way to break container consciousness is to cut the sides of the root ball in three or four places and spread the roots apart when the plant is set out. Although this procedure looks radical to the uninitiated, it's the path to horticultural health.

Churches and ministers can become too comfortable in their settings also. Especially if they have some success in ministry, they may spend the rest of their lives moving in the familiar cycles. Container consciousness is an establishment mind-set. The past has become so comfortable that the future becomes expendable. That tragic conclusion, imperceptibly and inexorably, begins to embalm institutions. Only radical repotting can save traditionalized congregations and give them a strategic orientation toward the future.

SURVIVING FEASIBLY

The book of Revelation presents a different challenge for strategists. Revelation represents an exception to the normal strategic cycle of focus, flexibility, and future-orientation. Why? Because Revelation describes a crisis of cosmic proportions. Only two biblical books—Revelation and Esther—depict dire situations in which the survival of the faithful is on the line. In Revelation sick religion and sick government are allied against the church. Believers are under extreme pressure. When the stakes are so high, believers do what they can feasibly do with integrity to survive. Then they return to the focus with flexibility on the future action sequence.

Survival is a stern taskmaster. Dr. Moran, Winston Churchill's personal physician during World War II, feared every soldier would eventually buckle under the pressure of battle. Consequently, he saw courage as willpower—the grit to keep on keeping on. When pressure is intense, leaders need a strategic target to return to after the trauma has passed. Feasibility and faithfulness may be the orders of the day in the face of crisis. But focus, flexibility, and a future-orientation will guide leaders over the long haul.

TIME-SPECIFIC STRATEGIES

Leaders soon learn that strategy is time-specific. Some strategic moves match specific situations, and other strategies fit different circumstances. Focus fits new ministry launches when scarce resources and energies must be carefully directed. Flexible strategies match up with eras of expansion when innovation and timing are at a premium. Futuristic strategies are required when tomorrow is in jeopardy. Feasibility strategies are tailored to persons and organizations in dire straits. Feasibility approaches are temporary. Focus, flexibility, and future-orientation are designed to keep us moving creatively toward God's best possibilities for us.

CHANGING THE WORLD

Focused, flexible, and future-oriented persons can make a difference in a congregation and in a culture. And it doesn't take many committed persons to create change. In fact, a strategic minority can change the world. Judith Bardwick claims, "For strategy to succeed it must anticipate, create, and guide change and create commitment in the organization's members."[12] We've seen the impact of revolutionary groups throughout history. Sociologist Robert Bellah believes that if a small segment of a society—perhaps as few as two percent—shares a new vision of what that society can become, they can change their world.[13] That's what Jesus and his followers did.

Strategic leaders leaven, light, and season their surroundings. Their vision brings meaning to others who are searching for direction and fulfillment. God's kingdom, fresh opportunities offered by the Holy Spirit, and hope for tomorrow are the bright spotlights religious leaders use to set the pace in the Information Age.

PART THREE

SETTING SAIL
ON THE LEADERSHIP
VOYAGE INTO THE FUTURE

CHAPTER 6

Meaning-Making 101

L eading today's church is a lot like mastering the trapeze—
it's learning how to hold on, when to let go, and why the
whole process is so breathtaking! To lead well, now or in
the future, requires the "how's" of basic skills, the "when's" of
strategic timing, and the "why's" in the process of discovering
meaning. Many church leaders have built an impressive skill
array. Some have, often by native intuition, developed a strategic
touch. Few have become meaning makers. But now is the era for
those among us who become meaning makers to train ourselves
and to step forward.

MEANING-MAKING 101:
COURSE OVERVIEW

We haven't been schooled in making meaning in communities
of faith. Why don't we design a new course for leaders called
"Meaning-Making 101"? Then we can explore the behaviors of
leadership for the Information Age in a figurative laboratory.
Given the new shapes of leadership, how exactly is meaning
made? That's the key question. The answer? Meaning emerges
from leader-follower interactions when—together—we (1) create community connections, (2) orient teams to directional realities, and (3) anchor groups emotionally.

Leaders wear many hats and fill many roles, especially when they're trying to make sense out of a given set of circumstances. Meaning makers and meaning seekers are natural allies. Interpreters who make sense of the world serve as scouts and guides, as pathfinders and trailblazers, for those who are only beginning the meaning-making journey. Meaning makers act as compasses, gyroscopes, and rudders to stabilize their followers.

Leaders function in several pivotal roles in order to decipher information and make meaning. Let's catalog and describe each of these meaning-generating initiatives in more detail. Let's discover and define the actions and roles that are shaping the leadership river during our unique time in history. This meaning-making laboratory introduces us to a fresh approach to contemporary leadership.

MEANING-MAKING 101A: A COMMUNITY BUILDING LABORATORY

First, leaders serve as community builders. Such people identify patterns of connectedness.[1] Community building guides are pattern finders—finding patterns in information, patterns in relationships, patterns in group values. We weave varied, seemingly random pieces of information into larger frameworks of understanding. We link people together into teams, groups, and communities. We connect with followers' beliefs and express the dreams and desires in those values in ways that galvanize and move the group. In short, leaders are the looms for meaning making.

Meaning emerges through the connections we make with and within our anchoring group. Meaningful relationships serve as a magnetic field for our lives and orient our energies. Interpreters who make sense of life help us discover a secure sense of belonging to a like-minded group and interpret our linkages to the larger world.

Meaning Making and Community Building

One cluster of leadership roles helps followers build community. We make connections—relational and conceptual—within our group and beyond our group. Recognizing patterns of connectedness helps our group members make sense of the world.

Community Building Leader Actions

IDENTIFY PATTERNS   DESCRIBE CONTEXTS
FAMILIARIZE NEW   LINK CAUSE-EFFECT
CREATE INTERSECTIONS

Leaders exercise initiative in community building at several critical points in order to make meaning:

1. Meaning makers *identify patterns* between ideas, information, and incidents. Leaders recognize the ebb-and-flow and the contours of the situation; more important, we see how things fit together and merge into new configurations.
2. Meaning-making leaders *describe life's idea and interpersonal contexts* for our followers. Such guides always understand the importance of knowing our leadership river before we try to master the shape of that river. When asked how the American moon shot engineers and space explorers planned and launched their work, that group's coordinator replied, "First we found the moon." Context is crucial for leadership success.
3. Such interpreters also make time-related connections; we *familiarize the new* by blending the old with the new and by anchoring the now in the then. Leaders provide continuity frames for between-the-times eras by showing what deserves to be preserved from the past and by creating what's required of us for healthy futures.
4. Leaders *link cause-effect* by connecting stimuli and responses, problems and solutions, questions and answers. Impacts from previous decisions as well as implications of future choices link causes and effects.

5. Meaning makers *create intersections* by providing settings for persons to meet informally and for ideas to mix in unpressured settings. Meeting places—campfires, coffee breaks, clubhouses, porches, meal tables, computer screens—have been opportunities for guides to build communities and make meaning from the beginning of time.

Community Building Leader Roles

NAMER/IDENTIFIER
INTERPRETER/TRANSLATOR
CONNECTOR/COORDINATOR
COVENANTOR/AGREEMENT ARCHITECT
SYSTEM DECODER/CONTEXTUALIZER

There are are several fundamental roles leaders fill when we make meaning by building communities:

1. The *namer/identifier* role in meaning making provides cognitive categories to pinpoint the distinguishing character of a person or group. There is power in naming and identifying phenomena. Naming was taken seriously in the Bible; a person's name was seen as a reflection of character. In the early church, the ability to name a demon gave the namer power over it and opened the door for exorcism.

2. The *interpreter/translator* role puts unclear relationships and situations into understandable terms, describes the unknown, and clarifies or explains what has not been previously decoded.

3. The *connector/coordinator* role creates bonds, links people to others, combines facts in creative ways, unifies different opinions and personalities, and correlates diverse concepts.

4. The *covenantor/agreement architect* role weaves accords, promises, and pacts into lasting bonds of teamwork and cooperation.

5. The *contextualizer/system decoder* role explores the webs of history, frames situations, reads conditions, identifies norms of behavior, and links networks of relationships.

MEANING-MAKING 101B: A TEAM ORIENTEERING LABORATORY

Second, leaders serve as team orienteers. Map readers first find the arrow pointing toward the north. Then the remainder of the map can be interpreted. Likewise, leaders orient us. We point to true north. Leaders see what's going on in their group, tell the truth, and give names to values and phenomena that haven't been labeled before. Such people are spiritual, moral, and emotional compasses for their followers.

Meaning occurs when we jointly define our group's direction, set our rudders for the true north of that direction, and steer deliberately toward our reality. Working purposefully and intentionally for our goals is a basic ingredient in meaning making. Our intentions must be transformed into actions. Otherwise, leaders suffer from "intention deficit disorder." Leaders who make sense of life act to achieve their group's religious vision.

Meaning Making and Team Orienteering

This second cluster of meaning-making roles for leaders enables us to express our intentionality. As Max DePree claims, leaders "define reality." [2]

A newspaper editor once sent a new reporter to cover a major sporting event. The cub reporter returned shortly without a story. "Why don't you have a story?" asked the frustrated editor. "The stadium collapsed," was the reply. "Then why didn't you write about that event?" inquired the puzzled editor. "Because that wasn't my assignment!" answered the young reporter. Reality had escaped the cub reporter. Folks who can only spot large-scale happenings when they are specifically assigned to those events aren't likely to become reporters—or leaders—are they?

Orienteering as an avenue for meaning making calls for an array of leader actions. Several of these actions are "just a little bit more" initiatives. Meaning makers simplify the complex just a little bit more, focus attention just a little bit more, and solve riddles just a little bit more. Effectiveness in leadership, especially when orienting to reality, is often just a matter of degree of initiative.

Team Orienteering Leader Actions

ORIENT TO COMPASS	TELL TRUTH
NARROW HORIZONS	SIMPLIFY COMPLEX
REFRAME QUESTION	FOCUS ATTENTION
SOLVE RIDDLES	EMBODY SYMBOLS

GIVE HOPE

1. Leaders are orienteers. Meaning makers are those rare persons who point the direction, choose the course, and *orient others to north on the compass.*

2. Meaning makers *tell the truth.* Those who are leaders preach what we practice and practice what we preach. Our credibility rests on accurate readings of and sharing of facts and perceptions as well as on consistent actions.

3. Meaning makers *narrow horizons* when we focus the group's attention on a specific problem rather than allowing the group to become overwhelmed by every potential problem that could appear. These targeting actions limit distractions and connect problem-solving energy with the most basic challenge under investigation at this point in time.

4. Leaders *simplify the complex.* Meaning making requires us to cut through the haze, tune out the static, and streamline the complicated and puzzling. Otherwise, we get distracted by the trees and never find the forest.

5. *Reframing questions* is a basic avenue for making sense of our world. Reframing takes a difficult or overpowering dilemma, rotates it, and approaches it from a fresh angle. This technique is illustrated by a poster I saw recently. When the Israelite army encountered Goliath, they said, "He's so big we'll never kill him!" But David reframed the issue and completely changed the perspective: "He's so big I can't miss him!"

6. Team orienteers *focus attention* by targeting the essential and bypassing the peripheral. Those who interpret heed

the heart of the matter and spotlight only the core issues. We train the cross-hairs of our sights on one opportunity at a time.

7. Meaning makers *solve riddles* and unravel mysteries. Puzzles challenge all of us, but leaders search out the secrets and peer deliberately into the unknown.

8. Leaders appreciate the symbolic elements of pacesetting and, consequently, *embody symbols*. New Testament commentators describe Jesus' triumphal entry into Jerusalem riding a beast of burden as an embodied parable. What better way to demonstrate that he was a servant, not a warrior king?

9. There's no more crucial function for a meaning maker than to *give hope to others*. In the midst of despair, leaders speak of the future, identify opportunities, and leave visionary doors ajar. When paradigms shift and the culture cycles back to zero, only hopeful guides can turn back chaos and despair.

Leaders serve several pivotal roles as orienteers, direction finders, and reality discerners. Note some of these roles below.

Team Orienteering Leader Roles

TARGETER/RANGE FINDER
PROBLEM DEFINER/SOLUTION SEEKER
DETECTIVE/PROBER
MIRROR/REFLECTOR
DIAGNOSTICIAN/CATEGORIZER
VISIONARY/MYTH MANAGER
FRAMER/DESIGNER
IMAGE MAKER/STORYTELLER
THEORY BUILDER/OPTION TESTER

1. The *targeter/range finder* role asks "which?" and then "how far?" Finding the bull's-eye, steadily staying on the mark, and intending to pursue singular ends are basic ways reality is kept in the leader's viewfinder.

2. The *problem definer/solution seeker* role frames questions to be answered, specifies obstacles to be overcome, and

pinpoints puzzles to be solved. Ends and means stay linked in this process.

3. The *detective/prober* role inquires and searches for clues, inspects and investigates answers, and scrutinizes and scouts for proofs.

4. The *mirror/reflector* role holds phenomena up for additional examination, deeper reflection, increased angles of approach, and new revelations.

5. The *diagnostician/categorizer* role detects dynamics, recognizes circumstances, and distinguishes the key features of groupings, systems, or classifications.

6. The *visionary/myth manager* role identifies ideals and imagined possibilities to be expressed in realistic images and practical actions.

7. The *framer/designer* role shapes patterns, structures situations, formulates strategies, devises aims, fashions key purposes, and maps a range of options.

8. The *image maker/storyteller* role expands comprehension by drawing mental pictures and creating motivating visions through metaphors, illustrations, parables, anecdotes, slogans, and analogies.

9. The *theory builder/option tester* role tests hypotheses, analyzes assumptions, probes principles, and narrows alternatives in order to craft new possibilities.

MEANING-MAKING 101C: A GROUP ANCHORING LABORATORY

Third, leaders serve as group anchors. Or, stated differently, leaders are circuit breakers.[3] Leaders steady our group in times of high anxiety and, thereby, lessen the apprehensions of the group. Rather than overreacting, leaders slow the rush, clear the muddle, calm the uncertainty, make peace, and ease tension. We break the cycles of panic and fear by maintaining a nonanxious presence. In other words, leaders avoid paradigm panic, the urge to apply the quick fix to anxiety-provoking situations whether or not our repair efforts fit the need.

Meaning Making and Group Anchoring

Meaning is more apt to emerge in groups when leaders stand firm emotionally. Instead of running for the hills in the face of uncertainty, guides "stick with it." Interpreters who make sense of life have a central vision, focus our energies like a laser on that goal, give clear reasons for our actions, and don't deviate from our long-term direction. We discover congruence and live harmoniously when we align our purposes for living with our feelings, thoughts, and actions and behave accordingly. Life makes more sense and is more peaceful when we sort out our core values from peripheral concerns, act in accord with our deepest strivings, and persevere.

Group Anchoring Leader Actions

SLOW RUSH   CLARIFY MUDDLE
CALM UNCERTAINTY   FREEZE THE FLEETING   PLAY
DEPERSONALIZE DISAGREEMENTS
MAINTAIN A NONANXIOUS PRESENCE

1. Meaning makers *slow the rush* of life so that issues can soak. Then, seekers for meaning aren't as likely to be swept away by the floods of information or the fast pace of living. Calling a strategic time-out buys time for sense to be discovered.

2. Leaders *clarify the muddle* of information overload. It's easy to become bewildered by the confusing mix of choices and to need someone to help us unravel the tangles in our minds.

3. Meaning makers *calm uncertainties.* When faced with tough, murky decisions and an avalanche of data, it's natural to freeze up and to go into future shock. Leaders soothe our misgivings and allay our doubts by staying calm, cool, composed, and unruffled.

4. Leaders *freeze the fleeting.* Meaning making becomes

more difficult on the fly. Guides push the pause button and freeze frame the fast-moving world for us.

5. Meaning makers *play.* We enjoy new ideas, novel settings, interesting people, and challenging problems. We know that creative solutions bubble out of relaxed, playful interactions and are willing to play at our work.

6. Leaders *depersonalize disagreements.* We are clear that polarization grows out of personalizing blame. Rather, we use the passion of conflict to separate problems from people and to solve the problems.

7. Interpreters *maintain a nonanxious presence.* Knowing who we are, understanding what our values are, and having calculated our stake in an issue help us to remain more objective in the face of frustrations and confrontations. Groups are helped in finding their way if their leaders know their own way.

As group anchors, leaders fill some critical roles in keeping the group on an even keel. Scan these roles in the descriptions below.

Group Anchoring Leader Roles

STRESS MANAGER/TENSION EASER
CONFLICT MEDIATOR/PEACEMAKER
VALUES CLARIFIER/EVALUATOR
CENTERED BELIEVER/STABILIZER
MUDDLER/FELLOW PILGRIM

1. The *stress manager/tension easer* role helps groups "count to ten" before reacting, monitors groups' pressure points and anxiety levels, and uses structure and the changes-of-pace of humor and storytelling to lessen strain in the group.

2. The *conflict mediator/peacemaker* role turns friction, troublemaking, dissension, and strife on its head. With listening, diplomacy, mediation, arbitration, and sometimes confrontation, harmony is restored and energy refocused.

3. The *values clarifier/evaluator* role aids groups' attempts to understand their deepest values, evaluate how closely they

are adhering to the things they treasure, and operate from their bedrock principles.

4. The *centered believer/stabilizer* role searches for the core beliefs of a group, orients the group around those themes, and uses those convictions to root group actions and to pass along its viewpoints.

5. The *muddler/pilgrim* role accepts ambiguity and explores life's pioneering issues within the context of others' supportive companionship.

DRAWING MEANING MAPS

What accessible tools are available for church leaders to use in guiding persons or groups in the search for meaning? Asking thoughtful questions may be our most basic approach. Have you noticed how often Jesus answered a question with another question? Questions provoke thought. They stimulate a sorting process that opens the door for the discovery of breakthroughs in meaning. Meaning-making leaders ask "thought-full" questions and gently keep conversations flowing into deeper and deeper discoveries. In other words, leaders create "meaning maps" with gentle, well-crafted questions.

What do "meaning maps" look like? How do we move toward an understanding of meaning? The pilgrimage for meaning in our lives explores at least four directions—inward, outward, upward, and onward.

Listed below are clusters of inquiries leaders can use to help us, and others, examine sources of meaning in our lives.[4] The "inward cluster" deals with our internal yearnings, reflective memories, realities, and failures. The "outward cluster" explores our external network of meaningful relationships and arenas for action. The "upward cluster" opens up the vertical dimension of our lives. The "onward cluster" targets the directions and goals of our futures. The quest for answers to the fundamental question, "What do you want to do with your life?" makes meaning by stimulating insight and creating choices.[5]

Inward Meaning Maps

1. From which accomplishments do you take most satisfaction?
2. What option in life interests you now?
3. What do you dream about most?
4. With what regret do you continue to struggle?
5. When are you most joyous?
6. What fear holds you back?

Outward Meaning Maps

1. Who affirmed you most as a child and youth?
2. Which relationship is most important to you?
3. Who renews and refreshes you?
4. To whom do you need to say "I love you"?
5. Who has mentored you best?
6. Who is most likely to name you as their mentor?

Upward Meaning Maps

1. When have you felt most blessed?
2. When have you experienced a breakthrough in spiritual growth?
3. What belief is so central to you that I'll never fully understand you until I am aware of that core belief?
4. What is your deepest value?
5. When do you feel your God-given creativity is most stimulated?
6. What do you hope for most keenly in your future?

Onward Meaning Maps

1. When do you feel most fulfilled in ministry?
2. What is your calling in life?
3. What are your primary goals for the future?
4. What is your mission statement?
5. What do you hope for?

These and other clarifying questions help us identify those webs of meaning we humans hunger for. Our theological convictions both grow out of our quest for God's purposes in our lives, as well as from our desire to solidify those basic beliefs. This search for common sense has happened across all eras of the church's history.

MEANING-MAKING 101: FINAL EXAM

In the ebbing era, Industrial Agers have complained of meaninglessness—no goals, no sense of responsibility, or no inner moorings. Such a sense of aimlessness is a problem for Information Agers too. Why? Making meaning, in the perspective of time and history, creates continuity. Meaning becomes our ongoing search for the flow of our individual and group lives—what has happened to us, what is happening to us, and what's likely to happen to us.

Meaning is that rare commodity that's colloquially termed "common sense." Humans find meaning, then, through community building and pattern finding, by means of orienteering and defining reality, and by anchoring our groups and ourselves emotionally. We need a stabilizing sense of continuity with our pasts, presents, and futures; we want to relate the parts of our value systems to the whole; we try to inform the unknown with the familiar; we strive to move beyond raw information to understanding. These are fundamental approaches religious leaders use in groups to point followers toward meaning within the faith community.

CONNECTIVE THEOLOGY
FOR CONGREGATIONAL LEADERS

Let's sum up our theological view of leadership by featuring some connective principles and pictures. These perspectives match the demands of an interactive, systemic world. With meaning making as a foundation for leadership, we can now identify two basic resources for religious leaders: (1) some key understandings of leadership in social systems[6] and (2) some rich pictures of the church in the New Testament. Connective, networking assumptions of the Information Age grow out of relationships between leaders and followers. When these insights are coupled with the Church's affirmations about itself, meaning-making leadership approaches emerge.[7] Together, they provide a theological framework for congregational leaders.

Connectional Leadership Principle: Leaders rely on partner-ally followers. Leaders without followers are leaders only in our own minds. To our chagrin, we discover we are marching at the front of one-person columns. Connective leaders see followers as colleagues, not second-class or lower status persons.

Connective Theological Picture: Partnership images abound in the New Testament's discussions of the church. These word pictures focus on the relationship between Christ and believers. Especially in Paul's writings, "we-with" language is commonly used to describe partner-ally relationships. We live with (2 Corinthians 7:3), have been baptized with (Colossians 2:12), suffer with (Romans 8:17), are crucified with (Romans 6:6), die with (2 Corinthians 7:3), are buried with (Romans 6:4), are raised with (Ephesians 2:6 and Colossians 3:1), are made alive with (Ephesians 2:5 and Colossians 2:13), will be glorified with (Romans 8:17), and will rule with Christ (2 Timothy 2:12). Additionally, believers are shown as linked together as fellows in prison (Romans 16:7), work (Romans 16:21 and Colossians 4:11)), servanthood (Colossians 1:7 and 4:7), citizenship (Ephesians 2:19), and warfare (Philippians 2:25). Just as believers are partners with Christ, so are leaders and followers natural allies in ministry.

Connective Leadership Principle: Leadership is a field of ongoing interactions and connections. Leaders build rich relationships between ourselves and our followers. We know relationships ebb and flow over time so we work to develop connections with trust, durability, and quality between ourselves and our followers.

Students of contemporary leadership are struck by the instabilities of leader-follower relationships. As one of my more cynical friends describes the contemporary pastorate, "Ministers run for public office every Sunday morning at eleven!" No wonder political science helps inform religious leaders. Both politicians and ministers relate to fickle constituencies. Relationships call for cultivation.

Connective Theological Picture: It's no accident that the New Testament brims with citizenship images of the church. For example, about one hundred times, Jesus refers to God's kingdom. Additionally, the New Testament refers to believers as a chosen people . . . a people belonging to God (1 Peter 2:9). The ministry of reconciliation through Christ is our mission as kingdom citizens; we are Christ's ambassadors (2 Corinthians 5:20), always representing our Lord and presenting our witness before the changeable court of public opinion. Leaders are stewards of the ebbs and flows of relationships and systems.

Connective Leadership Principle: Leaders live comfortably amid transitory events. The alliance between leaders and followers shifts constantly. The field of interaction has beginnings, middles, and ends—leadership is more like a handful of loose pearls than a necklace. So leadership happens and stops and starts again.

Connective Theological Picture: Since God is a trailblazer, One who is always setting the pace from the front of the pack, his followers stay on the move too. Christians are pilgrims who travel light. We stay ready to explore new territories. The Church is made up of people of "the way" (Acts 9:2; 19:9 and 23; 24:14 and 22). Leaders are comfortable with transitions.

Connective Leadership Principle: Leaders bank on the quality of interpersonal relationships. Leadership is "people work." This is a key difference between leadership and management. Leadership is a person-to-person relationship and relies on commitment; management is a position-to-position transaction and builds on command.

Connective Theological Picture: In the New Testament, the church is described as a family. Relationships in the faith family are graciously offered, freely chosen, and mutually nurtured. When pictured in family terms, churches are God's household (Ephesians 2:19) and are characterized by relationships akin to siblings (1 John 3:14-16 and Romans 8:29) and mates (Ephesians 5:25-27 and 2 Corinthians 11:2). Leaders recognize that relationships must be constantly nurtured.

Connective Leadership Principle: Leaders operate in unstructured territories, in unknown arenas. Bureaucracies develop policies and procedures, providing a path—sometimes more cynically called ruts—for folks in authority. Effective guides learn to move around blockages and jump out of ruts by going where no defined path has been mapped. When the arena is ill-defined, leaders go instead where there is no path and leave a trail.[8]

Connective Theological Picture: In the New Testament, churches are clearly presented as learning organizations. Edification is a constant theme. Jesus is seen as a teacher (John 1:38 and 49; John 3:2; Ephesians 4:11), followers are apprentices (Acts 6:1-70), and believers are to build each other up (1 Thessalonians 5:11). Leaders use the unknowns of life as tutors.

Connective Leadership Principle: Leaders have no "safety net" and must learn to deal with risk and uncertainty. When cultural paradigms shift, the world goes back to zero and all the rules have to be relearned. Ambiguity and chaos become the order of the day. When others are frozen by uncertainty, these interpreters transform our anxieties into actions, see risk as challenge, and make meaning.

Connective Theological Picture: Farming, a prevalent image for the church in the New Testament, is another high-risk endeavor. Many uncertainties exist in the fields and flocks. Still, church leaders are depicted as vineyard keepers (Matthew 20:1-16) and shepherds (Acts 20:28; Hebrews 13:20; 1 Peter 5:2; Revelation 7:17). Leaders learn quickly there are no guarantees in leadership.

Connective Leadership Principle: Leaders don't realistically expect everyone to follow. Followers are hard to find and harder to hold. Some potential followers choose never to ally with us. Others join our cause for a time and then fall by the wayside. Leaders realize how precious an ally is and attend to followers' interests carefully.

Connective Theological Picture: The New Testament frequently sees the Church metaphorically as a physical body. The body of Christ image is one of Paul's favorite descriptions of the Church. Christ is, of course, spotlighted as the head of the Church (Colossians 1:18-19 and Ephesians 5:23). Human bodies require care to remain healthy. These theological perspectives help congregational leaders function more comfortably in dynamic systems.

Connective Leadership Principle: Leaders help meaning emerge. Those who lead and their followers become of one mind when seizing an opportunity or solving a problem becomes a joint endeavor. When persons interpret information the same and find meaning the same, a bond is formed and a leadership alliance is forged for that point in time. Followers expect leaders to advance our common cause. Interpreters and our followers mirror each other and our joint dreams. Consequently, leaders reflect followers, and followers get the leaders we deserve.

Connective Theological Picture: Physical structures are often used to picture the Church in the New Testament. In fact, the Church is called God's building (1 Corinthians 3:9). Before modern architects can lay cornerstones (Ephesians 2:20) and use pillars and bulwarks (1 Timothy 3:15), the client and the creator must agree on a common vision for the structure. A "meeting of minds" creates meaning for that encounter.

Connective Leadership Principle: Leaders know both followers and leaders share a common frame of reference that binds us together. These people see the world's realities through our own peculiar lenses. Leaders can only describe the world we are able to see. If that world matches followers' interests and hopes, followers follow. When leaders no longer articulate followers' aspirations, followers go our own way and leaders continue our quest for allies.

Connective Theological Picture: God's people take God's covenant promises seriously. We are promise people who realize that the Exodus in the Old Covenant and Pentecost in the New Covenant drew believers together. God has redeemed the world and called and covenanted with us to be a redemptive minority for the majority of the world. Leaders build shared frames of reference around our central beliefs.

To sum up, leaders prepare for our specific time in history—the Information Age, a world that's systemic, interactive, interrelated, and interdependent. We ready ourselves for the next church—hopeful, flexible, and open to new challenges. A connective theology will help us lead in this culture and this church.

LEADERS FOR A CHANGING CHURCH IN A CHANGING WORLD

Tomorrow's leaders will need three basic understandings—the shape of the river—in order to lead well in an interactive environment. Since leadership is a team sport, followers will need to discern the same foundational truths also.

1. *Tomorrow's leaders and followers will understand our leadership context.* We will understand the Information Age

paradigm as well as global and local settings for leadership and ministry. We will know our times—like the sons of Issachar (1 Chronicles 12:32). Religious interpreters will know our world.

2. *Tomorrow's leaders and followers will understand self-development.* We will stretch and grow in terms of leadership stance, styles, and strategies. Religious leaders will know ourselves.

3. *Tomorrow's leaders and followers will understand meaning making.* We will make common sense by building communities, orienting teams, and anchoring groups. Religious leaders will know our Lord and our group.

These are shapes of the leadership river and keys to future leadership in our world and for our church. In our interactive era of history, the world is asking questions for which the church has answers. Let's speak up! Let's make meaning! Let's lead!

AFTERWORD

A Parable of Hope for Future Leaders

Permanent white water. That's the metaphor two prominent leadership theorists use to describe the constantly
uncertain, turbulent condition of our changing world.[1] In
truth, today's leaders are always caught in the chaos of the rapids.
For those of us who fear we are at risk of being swept out to sea
by the tides of change, hear a parable of hope!

White water enthusiasts have developed a new design for
kayaks. Shaped like a potato chip or a high-tech wing, slightly
concave on top, with a very thin profile and bubbles built in for
the kayaker's legs, these new squirt boats have a strange charac-
teristic—they barely float! They rely on the action of the surging
river to make them fly, or squirt, through the water.

These new kayaks require a seasoned boater. Unlike novice
river-runners whose strategy is simply to shoot the rapids wildly,
the new kayakers learn to read the river. Whether by formal
instruction or by experimental play, these skillful boaters navigate
river patterns adroitly. They have noted that white water combines two dynamics—masses of water that plunge over rocks
more or less straight down the riverbed and circular eddies that
swirl upstream along the edges of obstacles and shorelines. Upstream? Yes, upstream.

It's these upstream forces that allow the seasoned boaters to
read the river. They use the swirls to rest, gather themselves
physically and emotionally, and study the currents. In the froth of

the eddies, savvy kayakers slow, turn, stop, or even drift back upstream a bit. Skillfully "playing the river" is what sets expert boaters apart from the weekend amateurs.

Here's the clue from this parable for effective leaders in turbulent times. Read the river. Then enjoy the process of playing the river. Interpret the shape of the river. Experiment and adjust the relationships of leadership. Amid the white water of change, that's what effective leaders of the new world and the next church will do.

NOTES

Foreword: A Parable of Hope for Frustrated Leaders

1. Mark Twain, *Life on the Mississippi* (New York: Signet, 1980), 58-59.

1. Challenges of Leadership in a Postmodern World

1. In embryonic form, some of the material in this chapter appeared in an essay, "The Shape of the River: Training Young Leaders for a Changing World," in *Leadership for a Changing World,* a booklet of three winning essays compiled for the twenty-fifth anniversary celebration of Center for Creative Leadership on June 13, 1995, in Greensboro, N.C.

2. Howard Gardner, *Leading Minds: An Anatomy of Leadership* (New York: BasicBooks, 1995), 298-302.

3. Larry C. Spears, ed., *Reflections on Leadership: How Robert K. Greenleaf's Theory of Servant-Leadership Influenced Today's Top Management Thinkers* (New York: John Wiley & Sons, 1995).

4. Joseph L. Badaracco, Jr. and Richard R. Ellsworth, *Leadership and the Quest for Integrity* (Boston: Harvard Business School, 1989).

5. Larry R. Donnithorne, *The West Point Way of Leadership* (New York: Currency Doubleday, 1994).

6. Jay A. Conger and Associates, *Spirit at Work* (San Francisco: Jossey-Bass, 1994).

7. James M. Kouzes and Barry Z. Posner, *Credibility* (San Francisco: Jossey-Bass, 1993).

8. James M. Kouzes and Barry Z. Posner, *The Leadership Challenge* (San Francisco: Jossey-Bass, 1987).

9. Max DePree, *Leadership Is an Art* and *Leadership Jazz* (New York: Doubleday, 1992).

10. James O'Toole, *Leading Change* (San Francisco: Jossey-Bass, 1995).

11. Stephen R. Covey, *The Seven Habits of Highly Effective People* (New York: Simon and Schuster, 1989).

12. Wess Roberts, *Leadership Secrets of Attila the Hun* (New York: Warner Communications, 1985).

13. Laurie Beth Jones, *Jesus, CEO* (New York: Hyperion, 1995).

14. Emmett C. Murphy with Michael Snell, *The Genius of Sitting Bull* (New York: Prentice-Hall, 1993).

15. Don T. Phillips, *Lincoln on Leadership* (New York: Warner, 1992).

16. Robert D. Dale, *Pastoral Leadership* (Nashville: Abingdon Press, 1986) and *Good News from Great Leaders* (Washington, D.C.: Alban, 1992).

17. See Henry Mintzberg, "Crafting Strategy," *Harvard Business Review,* Reprint No. 87407 (1987) and Bruce D. Henderson, "The Origin of Strategy," *Harvard Business Review* (November-December 1989): 139-143.

18. Tom Peters, *Liberation Management* (New York: Knopf, 1992), 575-76.

19. Michel Robert, *Strategy Pure and Simple* (New York: McGraw-Hill, 1993).

20. Robert D. Dale, *Leading Edge: Leadership Strategies from the New Testament* (Nashville: Abingdon Press, 1996).

21. Linda Smircich and Gareth Morgan, "Leadership: The Management of Meaning," *Journal of Applied Behavioral Science* 18, no. 3: 257-73; and Wilfred H. Drath and Charles J. Palus, *Making Common Sense* (Greensboro, N.C.: Center for Creative Leadership, 1994).

22. Jean Lipman-Blumen, *The Connective Edge: Leading in an Interdependent World* (San Francisco: Jossey-Bass, 1996).

23. Gerald Nadler and Shozo Hibino with John Ferrell, *Creative Solution Finding: The Triumph of Full-Spectrum Creativity over Conventional Thinking* (Rocklin, Calif.: Prima Publishing, 1995).

24. Howard Gardner, *Leading Minds: An Anatomy of Leadership* (New York: BasicBooks, 1995), 296.

25. Joel Arthur Barker, *Paradigms: The Business of Discovering the Future* (New York: HarperBusiness, 1992), 164.

26. Stephen R. Covey, *Principle-Centered Leadership* (New York: Summit Books, 1990), 19.

27. Gordon Allport, *The Individual and His Religion* (New York: Macmillan, 1950), 20.

28. Price Pritchett, *New Work Habits for a Radically Changing World* (Dallas: Pritchett & Associates, 1994).

29. Ibid., 15.

2. Religious Leaders for Tomorrow's Church

1. Charles Trueheart, "Welcome to the Next Church," *Atlantic Monthly* 278, no. 2 (August 1996): 37-58.

2. Margaret Mead, *Culture and Commitment: A Study of the Generation Gap* (Garden City, N.Y.: Natural History Press/Doubleday, 1970), xx.

3. Ibid.

4. C. Jeff Woods, *Congregational Megatrends* (Washington, D.C.: Alban, 1996), 12.

5. Loren Mead, *The Once and Future Church* (Bethesda, Md.: Alban, 1991), 8-18.

6. Paul M. Diettrich, "What Time Is It?" *Transformation* (Center for Parish Development) I, no. 3 (Fall 1993): 1-7.

7. Kennon Callahan, *Effective Church Leadership* (San Francisco: Harper & Row, 1990), 13-21.

8. Alvin and Heidi Toffler, *Creating a New Civilization* (Atlanta: Turner, 1995).

9. James Bailey, *After Thought: The Computer Challenge to Human Intelligence* (New York: BasicBooks, 1996).

10. Margaret Jo Wheatley, *Leadership and the New Science* (San Francisco: Berrett-Koehler, 1992), 43.

11. Howard Gardner, *Leading Minds: An Anatomy of Leadership* (New York: BasicBooks, 1995), 292.

12. For these perspectives, see John Shelton Reed, *The Enduring South* (Chapel Hill: University of North Carolina Press, 1986) and *1001 Things Everyone Should Know About the South* (New York: Doubleday, 1996).

13. Max DePree, *The Art of Leadership* (New York: Doubleday, 1989), 9.

14. Edwin H. Friedman, *Generation to Generation* (New York: Guilford Press, 1985), 209.

15. Tim O'Brien, *The Things They Carried* (Boston: Houghton Mifflin, 1990), 40.

16. Viktor E. Frankl, *Man's Search for Meaning* (New York: Washington Square Press, 1959), 121.

17. Norman Maclean, *A River Runs Through It* (Chicago: University of Chicago Press, 1976), 1.

18. Ibid., 95-96, 104.

19. Linda-Marie Delloff, "Outreach Opportunity Puts Theology in Action," *Progressions: A Lilly Endowment Occasional Report* 5, no. 1 (February 1995), 9.

3. Values: Discovering Meaning Through Leadership Stance

1. Lee Carolynn Jacobson, *Pitterpat* (Norfolk, Va.: Hampton Roads Publishing Company, 1994).

2. Ernest Mosley, from a lecture entitled "Leading with a Towel," 1989 Northcutt Lectures on Pastoral Ministries, Southwestern Baptist Theological Seminary, Fort Worth, Texas.

4. Versatility: Broadening Meaning Through Leader Styles

1. For a model of leadership as mission, see Robert D. Dale, *To Dream Again* (Nashville: Broadman, 1981).

2. For an example of leadership as morale, see Robert D. Dale, *Keeping the Dream Alive* (Nashville: Broadman, 1988).

3. Robert E. Kaplan, *Forceful Leadership and Enabling Leadership: You Can Do Both* (Greensboro, N.C.: Center for Creative Leadership, 1996), 24.

4. This section is based on Kaplan's wise treatment in *Forceful Leadership and Enabling Leadership.*

5. Edwin Shneidman, *Voices of Death* (New York: Harper & Row, 1980), 1-6.

6. Leslie Miller, "Faith in God at Heavenly Heights," *USA Today* (December 21, 1994): D1.

5. Vision: Focusing Meaning Through Leader Strategies

1. Leighton Ford, *Transforming Leadership* (Downers Grove, Ill.: InterVarsity Press, 1991), 71.

2. Michael Treacy and Frederick D. Wiersema, *Discipline of Market Leaders* (Reading, Mass.: Addison-Wesley, 1995).

3. Norm Abram, *Measure Once, Cut Twice: Lessons from a Master Carpenter* (Boston: Little, Brown and Company, 1996).

4. Robert D. Dale, *Leading Edge* (Nashville: Abingdon Press, 1996).

5. Judith M. Bardwick, "Peacetime Management and Wartime Leadership," in

Frances Hesselbein, Marshall Goldsmith, and Richard Beckhard, eds., *The Leader of the Future* (San Francisco: Jossey-Bass, 1996), 134.

6. Henry Mintzberg, "Crafting Strategy," *Harvard Business Review*, Reprint No. 88407 (1987).

7. I developed this model of strategic leadership from a New Testament perspective in *Leading Edge*.

8. Ford, *Transforming Leadership*, 53.

9. Robert D. Dale, *To Dream Again* (Nashville: Broadman, 1981), 38-40.

10. Sibella C. Giorello, "Seeking His Deliverance," *Richmond [Virginia] Times-Dispatch* (January 24, 1997): C1, C3.

11. Donna C. L. Prestwood and Paul Schumann, Jr., "Seven New Principles of Leadership," *The Futurist* (January-February 1996): 68.

12. Judith M. Bardwick, *The Leader of the Future*, 136.

13. Robert N. Bellah, Richard Madsen, William M. Sullivan, Ann Swidler, and Steven M. Tipton, *Habits of the Heart: Individualism and Commitment in American Life* (Berkeley: University of California, 1985), 181-85.

6. Meaning-Making 101

1. Margaret J. Wheatley, *Leadership and the New Science* (San Francisco: Barrett-Koehler, 1992), 43.

2. Max DePree, *Leadership Is an Art* (New York: Doubleday, 1989), 9.

3. Edwin H. Friedman, *Generation to Generation* (New York: Guilford Press, 1985), 209.

4. The questions below are adapted from the logotherapy approach of Paul R. Welter, *Counseling and the Search for Meaning* (Waco: Word, 1987), 65-70.

5. Lawrence LeShan, *You Can Fight for Your Life* (New York: M. Evans and Co., 1980), 140.

6. Warren Blank, *The Nine Natural Laws of Leadership* (New York: AMACOM, 1995).

7. Robert D. Dale, *Sharing Ministry with Volunteer Leaders* (Nashville: Convention, 1986).

8. Blank, *The Nine Natural Laws of Leadership*, 17.

Afterword

1. Peter Vaill, *Managing as a Performing Art* (San Francisco: Jossey-Bass, 1989), 2; and Charles J. Palus, "Permanent White Water: Playing with the Metaphor," *Issues & Observations* 15, no. 1 (1995): 7-9.